LARGE-PRINT
GREAT BIG CROSSWORDS™

KAPPA Books

Visit us at www.kappabooks.com

Copyright ©2022 by Kappa Books Publishers, LLC.
No part of this book may be reproduced or copied without written permission of the publisher.
All rights reserved. Printed in the UNITED STATES OF AMERICA.

PUZZLE 1

ACROSS

1 Confidence
6 Like some mattresses
10 Induce
13 Sailing on the water
14 Aunt or uncle
15 Breakfast in bed need
16 Bullfight bellow
17 Coffeepots for crowds
18 Soldier's address letters
19 Peddle
21 V preceders
22 Stare at rudely
23 Nabisco favorites
25 Observes
27 Shyness
29 Like a cherub
32 Mexican sauce
36 Asian land
37 Mr.'s mate
39 Race segments
40 "__ Little Teapot" (2 wds.)
41 "I __ Spell on You" (2 wds.)
43 Sold-out letters at a theater
44 Belfry dwellers
46 Allows to remain (2 wds.)
48 Single article
49 Giving a nudge
50 "__ Leaving Home"
51 Like candy

DOWN

1 Trial balloon
2 TV host Dahl
3 "Patience __ virtue" (2 wds.)
4 Ballet wear
5 Split __ (quibble)
6 Jack Sprat ate none
7 Mideast nation
8 Gathered crops
9 Certain elected officials
10 Resort south of Salt Lake City
11 Elvis Presley hit (3 wds.)
12 Comes after
20 Certain roofs
22 Faithful
24 Fa follower
26 Altitudes (abbr.)
28 Cheek feature
29 Courtroom excuses
30 Super Bowl III superstar
31 Pointy beard
33 Famous collie
34 Run at top speed
35 "I Feel __ Coming On" (2 wds.)
38 Pierces
42 Admit
45 Certain sweater sizes (abbr.)
47 Ram's dam

PUZZLE 2

ACROSS

1 Type of TV
7 High school course (abbr.)
10 Restless
11 Radio and television, e.g.
13 Appalled
14 Hymn endings
15 Tycoon Onassis, informally
16 "__ only a paper moon..."
17 Close a Windbreaker (2 wds.)
18 Summer home
20 Taboo things
21 Lacking warmth
22 Walk __ in my shoes (2 wds.)
24 Tonto's pal (3 wds.)
29 Krabappel and Mode
30 Chaplin's prop
31 Former Las Vegas casino
33 Sealy competitor
34 Triplets number
35 Lager alternative
37 Slumber site
38 "Green Eggs and Ham" author
39 Fancy spread
41 Blue Ribbon maker
42 Issue forth
43 Mrs., to a Mexican
44 Less bright

DOWN

1 Tut's title
2 Like good penmanship
3 German exclamation
4 Blotch
5 "Gorillas in the __"
6 Drama divisions
7 Expert
8 Comics blanket-carrier
9 Shocked sound
11 Corn oil brand
12 Cardinal's title
15 Part of CPA (abbr.)
19 Inactivity
20 Film lot figures (abbr.)
22 Landers and Jillian
23 __ culpa
25 Least normal
26 Rubbish
27 One going in
28 Prepare for a book report
31 Clip
32 Caribbean resort island
33 Break off
34 Cook's measures (abbr.)
35 Won easily
36 Tibetan monk
40 Chafe

PUZZLE 3

ACROSS

1 Real estate ad abbr.
5 Lobster's pincher
9 Talked romantically
10 Type of exercise
14 Clutches
15 Renovate
16 Pot starter
17 It follows Mar.
18 Sandwich shop
19 Merit
21 Wartime "meat"
22 Unlike Zeus
25 Compass dir.
26 Towing gp.
29 Start for scope or surgery
30 Driller's deg.
31 Special treatment, for short
32 Goodman and Burstyn
34 Twitches
36 Betrothed
40 Skeptic's comment
(2 wds.)
41 Ewe sound
42 Refrain syllables (2 wds.)
43 Football player
45 Squelched (2 wds.)
46 Dancer Fred
47 Readies, briefly
48 Pinocchio, for one
49 Take the car

DOWN

1 Pioneer Daniel
2 Blockheads
3 Cash in coupons
4 Hosp. figs.
5 Rug sprucer-upper (2 wds.)
6 Suggestive look
7 Dog's bark
8 Dictionary entries
9 Landlocked African country
11 Used a horn
12 "Treasure ___"
13 Church bells
17 "Sk8er Boi" singer Lavigne
20 Setting for "Julius Caesar"
23 Sports stadium
24 Lengthy
26 Famed Hun
27 Courtroom excuses
28 Regional speech tone
33 African expedition
35 Pilfer
37 Barred to outsiders
38 Run off to wed
39 Blocker et al.
41 Actress Theda
44 1002, to Claudius
45 May's season (abbr.)

PUZZLE 4

ACROSS

1 Beeper
6 Streisand of "Yentl"
12 Amazon's voice assistant
13 "Enough, __!"
15 Secretary of State Powell
16 Letter
17 Lab vessel (2 wds.)
19 Research org. (abbr.)
20 Burn superficially
22 Be able to buy
27 Lithe
31 Frivolous facts
32 Winter vehicle
33 Righteous
34 Women
35 Andes creature
38 Part of NYPD (abbr.)
41 Harry Potter's school
47 Musical
49 All
50 Metal-bearing mineral (2 wds.)
51 Turn yellow, as a banana
52 Alters a text
53 Summon

DOWN

1 International agreement
2 Burn plant
3 Sets
4 Go out
5 Rage
6 Thumper's deer friend
7 E.T., e.g.
8 Monopoly foursome (abbr.)
9 Encircled by enemy troops
10 Precipitate
11 Pts. of speech
14 Up until now
18 Meat inspection inits.
21 Festive gathering
22 Banking machine (abbr.)
23 To's partner
24 Balsam __
25 "Secret decoder ring" powder
26 Streamlet
28 Sundial's 3
29 Shirt size (abbr.)
30 Sounds of inquiry
32 Dross
36 Take __ look at (2 wds.)
37 Lawn tunnelers
38 551, in Cicero's day
39 "Jane __" (Bront°)
40 "Carrie" event
42 Had been
43 Tel __
44 Seized vehicle, informally
45 Hard journey
46 End of a 12/31 title
48 Opposite of pro

PUZZLE 5

ACROSS

1 Walks lamely
6 General Tom __
11 Sporty Chevy
12 Strictness
13 Belittled
14 Pertaining to a national group
16 Religious off-shoots
17 Dogie roper
18 Part of AKA
19 Rent
20 Head honcho, moneywise (abbr.)
21 552, to Caesar
23 Gentlemen
25 Challenge
28 Church officials
29 Fair-haired
30 Country's McEntire
31 "__ Are My Sunshine"
32 DDE's succes-sor
33 London baby buggy
37 Petted
40 "__ to be born..." (Eccle-siastes, 2 wds.)
41 Pointed sticks
42 __ de Havilland
43 Long-legged bird
44 President Reagan
45 College admin-istrators
46 Trumpet's kin

DOWN

1 Can wrapper
2 Apple products that debuted in 1998
3 Tusked mammal of the Ice Age
4 Corporate executive (abbr.)
5 Turf
6 Goody
7 Popular shows
8 Expressions of disgust
9 Mr. Peanut's accessory
10 Shorter
11 Mexican house
15 Use a bridge
17 Honolulu airport wear
19 Turned the lamp on
22 Mind-bending drug (abbr.)
23 Gp. that includes the Rockies
24 Adjusting
25 Bottomless pit
26 Coagulated
27 Mettle
28 Mouse sight-er's word
30 "Mayberry, __"
32 Jokes
34 Person on the other team
35 Talk __ a minute (2 wds.)
36 Fermented honey beverage
38 Gumbo pods
39 Sharp-edged
40 Outfielder Matty
42 Spherical body

PUZZLE 6

ACROSS

1 Ridicule
6 Provide warmth
10 Kid's musical instrument
11 __ Goose
14 As gentle as __ (2 wds.)
15 According to schedule (2 wds.)
16 Dormant
18 "The Sweetheart of __ Chi"
19 Spruce up
20 Republican party's inits.
22 Singe
23 Onassis, to friends
24 Fesses up
26 Mariner's dir.
27 Remove frost
28 TV schedule abbr.
31 Jared Kushner's spouse
32 Hoop lip
33 Singly
36 T-shirt size
37 __ jockey
38 Asserts as a fact
40 Least normal
42 Second selling
44 Tanker
45 Sports locales
46 Edie of "Nurse Jackie"
47 Invitation initials
48 London apartments

DOWN

1 Rink users
2 Thermal unit
3 Jason Bateman money-laundering series
4 Lively play
5 "It was nothing"
(3 wds.)
6 Certain insurance option (abbr.)
7 Eternities
8 House toppers
9 Leg part
12 Actress Stone
13 __ view mirror
17 Santo __
19 Dads
21 Tagged out a base runner (2 wds.)
24 Pt. of speech
25 Lipton beverage
28 Divide into thirds
29 Cozy wine-shops
30 "Better Call Saul" network
31 Natives of Ames
33 TV chef Moulton
34 No longer happening
35 Defeated contestant
37 Perry Mason's secretary
39 Bohemian, e.g.
41 Former phone feature
43 Psychic's skill (abbr.)

PUZZLE 7

ACROSS

1 The Boston __
5 Streamlet
9 "We __ amused" (2 wds.)
11 South African singer __ Makeba
13 Fraud
14 Develop
15 Make swollen
16 Boone or Webster
17 Slippery crea-
tures
18 Barn's adjunct
19 Quipsters
20 Root vegeta-bles
24 Become old
25 Like lather
27 '30s relief agency (abbr.)
28 Curvaceous
30 Con man's plan
31 They woo colleens
32 Like sore muscles
33 Employ incor-rectly
36 Home Depot rival
38 Publishes a book
39 Engines
40 Doohickey
41 Strong yearning
42 Pip
43 Sir's female counterpart

DOWN

1 Beverage from Sri Lanka (2 wds.)
2 Shaq et al.
3 Seacoast cities
4 Pig's digs
5 Keen competi-tion
6 Type of patch (hyph.)
7 "Darling __"
8 Bathe
9 Military jet's locale (abbr.)
10 Sir Walter __
11 Intermediate
12 Tormé or Brooks
18 Waits behind
19 Existed
21 Small caterpil-lar
22 Supplications
23 Anchorman Donaldson
25 Had a banquet
26 Born first
29 Dive
30 Canada's Nova __
32 Luau greeting
33 Car efficiency stat
34 Gershwin and Glass
35 __ order
37 Concorde's initials
39 "Rhoda" pro-duction co.

PUZZLE 8

ACROSS

1 Subject
6 Maple sweet stuff
11 Second tennis point
12 17-syllable poem
13 Religious text (2 wds.)
16 Prior, to a poet
17 "It's a sin to tell ___" (2 wds.)
18 "Born Free" feline
19 No ifs, ___, or buts
21 Cruel person
23 Spain's cont.
24 Rascals
26 Bedtime stories
28 Billionaire Jeff
30 Scrutinizes
31 Like a rainbow
32 Mentally healthy
33 Greek letter
34 Spot
36 Verdi opera
40 Egg-shaped
42 Cougar
44 Dip in liquid
45 Items in an old-time gym (2 wds.)
48 ___ panels
49 Deny
50 Make an attempt at (2 wds.)
51 Pours heavily

DOWN

1 Rosebush hazard
2 Greased
3 Nose around
4 "___ living" (2 wds.)
5 One-eyed monster
6 Not as outgoing
7 Bark
8 ___ of passage
9 Small, Hawaiian guitar
10 Seeks to accomplish
11 "Take ___ Train" (2 wds.)
14 Tractor-trailers
15 All ___ (attentive)
20 Medium or extra-large
22 Where the princes schooled
25 "Ugly Betty" magazine
27 Space
28 Most valiant
29 South American country
30 Loan installment
31 Particle
32 Made a web
35 Politician Agnew
37 Imam's religion
38 Numskulls
39 Church projection
41 Diva Pons
43 "...sting like ___" (2 wds.)
46 Lynx, e.g.
47 Candle count

ACROSS

1 Actor Buchanan
6 250, in old Rome
9 Bagel's sweeter cousin
10 Chooses
14 Remove evidence of
15 Seven Dwarfs' worksong (hyph.)
16 Salamander
17 Medicine chest staple
18 Corporate absorption
21 Swindle scheme
22 Moronic
24 Draft agcy.
25 Relevant
26 Contains
29 Sis's sibling
32 Everlasting
36 They light up rooms
39 Famed Hun
40 Partly cover
42 Also
44 Charm with attractions
45 Scorn
46 Defame
47 News sources
48 Wide shoe width
49 High-priced

DOWN

1 Adam's home
2 Scale start (3 wds.)
3 Nibbled, beaver-style
4 Where Vienna is
5 Delivery course (abbr.)
6 Third letters
7 Cuts off
8 Within the law, for short
10 Puppeteer ___ Lewis
11 Rock or O'Donnell
12 Slenderizes
13 Ballads
19 Dems.' foes
20 Kitchen or major ender
23 Guitarist Atkins
27 Museum's display
28 Small scrap
29 Glops
30 Come undone
31 Greek letter
33 Diminish to a point
34 Refer (to)
35 Actress ___ Metcalf
37 Sunkist fruit
38 Playground feature
41 Skipper's direction
43 Ginger ___
45 Certain sweater sizes (abbr.)

PUZZLE 10

ACROSS

1 Electroshock weapon
6 Stabs
11 Fidel of Cuba
12 Not active
13 NASA project (2 wds.)
16 Baseball's Griffey
17 Relative of etc. (2 wds.)
18 Glut
19 Inch forward
21 Role in "Casablanca"
23 Egyptian boy king
24 Weathercock
26 Zodiac ram
28 Teen talk
30 Holey footwear
31 Use a crane
32 Foolish people
33 Where military planes land (abbr.)
34 Rebuff
36 Pretense
40 Wine glass support
42 Slaughter of baseball
44 Wallach or Whitney
45 "Mamma Mia! __" (2018 film, 4 wds.)
48 Dubbed
49 Sifters
50 Messy people
51 Comic DeGeneres

DOWN

1 Used a VCR
2 "With __ in My Heart" (2 wds.)
3 Gateway Arch city (abbr.)
4 A Gardner
5 Cheering
6 Young women
7 Artist and musician Yoko __
8 Rules (abbr.)
9 Eccentric
10 Rodin pieces, e.g.
11 "Piece of __!"
14 Not vivid
15 National League team
20 Gabor and Perón
22 50+ org.
25 Picnic visitors
27 "Friends" character
28 Makes less hard
29 Broad-minded
30 Final railroad car
31 Corned beef __
32 Caroled
35 Is in want
37 Haul up
38 Visitor from another planet
39 Parts of hrs.
41 Post-it message
43 Jib
46 World Wide __
47 Toothpaste variety

PUZZLE 11

ACROSS

1 Collar stiffener
5 A la __
10 Fleet officer
13 Pirouette
14 Wrinkle, as paper
15 Picture puzzle
16 Pitcher __ Hamels
17 "__ cost ya!"
19 Arthur of "Maude"
20 Loafer tip
21 Presidential turndown
22 Playwright Hart
23 Spending binge
25 Very serious
27 Go down
29 Noisy, mischievous bird
31 Fop's neckwear
35 Sinise of "CSI: NY"
36 Run smoothly
38 "Ben-__" (Wallace)
39 Keats work
40 Dance instruction
41 __ dry eye in the house (2 wds.)
42 Actress Bialik
44 Clothed
46 Show a lot of feeling
47 Full-length motion picture
48 Recycle
49 Some report card grades

DOWN

1 One saying "cheese"
2 Fork point
3 Noah's __
4 New Haven alumnus
5 Keyboard combo __-Alt-Del
6 Overwhelm
7 Winner's prize
8 Most loyal
9 "Frozen" queen et al.
10 Bank holdings (abbr.)
11 Hang low
12 Piece of romaine (2 wds.)
18 Folk myth
21 Mondale, once
22 Prescriptions, for short
24 Uneasy
26 Wear down teeth
28 Strain flour
29 Monsieur's mate
30 Hendrix's "__ Experienced" (2 wds.)
32 Vocal group
33 __ space
34 Word in FTC
35 Private Pyle
37 Chose
40 Captain Hook's sidekick
41 Nick at __
43 "__ only a paper moon..."
45 Inventor's monogram

PUZZLE 12

ACROSS

1 Affirm confidently
5 Black-and-white whale
9 Sounds of surprise
12 Go by burro
13 Listen
14 Lincoln __
16 Ole Miss rival
17 "...maids all in __" (2 wds.)
18 "Beatles for Sale" cut (3 wds.)
20 "The __ Pokey" (kids' song)
22 Prius maker
23 "__ Day Now"
24 Over and over
27 In no way
28 Temerity
29 Phone download
32 Prepare to be knighted
33 Wanted poster initials
36 Purple flower
38 Heidi's holler
40 Tel Aviv citizens
43 Jai __
44 Business letter abbr.
45 Acting like Mt. Vesuvius
47 Froglike creature
48 River sediment
49 Hamburger roll
50 Added additions
51 Disapproving sounds

DOWN

1 Departure's opposite (abbr.)
2 IV x II
3 Cheeseboard selection
4 Kinsman
5 Buddy Holly hit (2 wds.)
6 Think logically
7 Responded to smelling salts (2 wds.)
8 Biblical mountain
9 Nebraska city
10 Marsh wader
11 Great __ Mountains
15 Be beholden to
19 Forlorn
21 New York baseballer
25 Most soft-hearted
26 Have life
29 Emulate Amelia Earhart
30 Certain gun
31 Entranceway
33 Unrehearsed, as a speech (hyph.)
34 Reeves of "The Matrix"
35 Adjust
37 Disembarks
39 Feedbag item
41 Purple flower
42 Mope
46 Touchdown's six, e.g. (abbr.)

PUZZLE 13

ACROSS

1 Melodramatic shout
5 Word in CIA (abbr.)
9 Historic age
12 Jolie's Croft
13 Egyptian river
14 Numerals (abbr.)
15 Gasoline, e.g.
16 Vacationers
18 Worldwide (abbr.)
19 Miner's paydirt
20 Word on a lo-cal beer can
21 Reverberating
23 "__ misty..." (2 wds.)
24 Aloha State
25 Bows
26 Honking bird
28 Stallone role
32 Military command (2 wds.)
36 Daredevil Knievel
37 Wickerwork materials
39 Former NBC late night host
40 Sound booster
41 Author Rendell
42 First
44 Tan, in fashion
45 Stubborn __ mule (2 wds.)
46 Hamlet, e.g.
47 Be an usher
48 Dover's state (abbr.)
49 Blend with a spoon
50 Cooking amts.

DOWN

1 Michael Caine role
2 Begin
3 Singer Franklin
4 Sickly looking
5 Banderas of "Evita"
6 Italian fashion company (2 wds.)
7 Detective's aid
8 "__ dern tootin' "
9 Navy officer
10 Decayed
11 Belongings
17 Net pro Nastase
22 "Othello" bad guy
25 Sugar source
27 Paper-fastening device
28 Insert film again
29 Reluctant
30 Servile
31 Internet journal
33 In repose (2 wds.)
34 Pasta toppings
35 Catch in a lure
38 Latches
40 Medical school course (abbr.)
43 Picks from a lineup (abbr.)

PUZZLE 14

ACROSS

1 Cries of surprise
5 Cooks' flavorings
10 Grips
12 Mr. T's squad (hyph.)
13 "Pssst! Over here!" (2 wds.)
14 Spoiled, as butter
16 Logger's tool
17 Cooking measurement (abbr.)
19 Neighbor of Texas (abbr.)
20 Cape Canaveral gp.
22 "Look out!" (hyph.)
24 Caesar's 54
25 Risk
27 __ layer
29 Breakfast choice (2 wds.)
33 "__ and Punishment"
34 Actress Harper
35 "Alley __" (comic strip)
36 Plaintiff
38 Price markers
42 London farewell (2 wds.)
44 Fussbudget
46 Diva's scarf
47 Talents
49 Venture forth
51 Cantor or Vedder
52 Della and Pee Wee
53 Distributed cards
54 Something essential

DOWN

1 Siri's counterpart
2 Actress Helen __
3 Jo March's youngest sister
4 X marks it
5 Groucho's brother
6 Airport monitor abbr.
7 Nevada gambling town
8 In-box filler
9 Beaming
10 Sleuth Charlie
11 Evanston, to Chicago, e.g.
15 Letterman et al.
18 Protection
21 Eden inhabitant
23 Coal scuttles
26 Iowa State's locale
28 Soap brand
29 Highlanders
30 Sounded like a frog
31 Dangerous current
32 More scary
37 Unnerved
39 Degrade
40 Pierced
41 __ Fifth Avenue
43 Alan of "The Aviator"
45 FBI agents (hyph.)
48 "__ Liza Jane"
50 Pollen gatherer

PUZZLE 15

ACROSS

1 Laughter sounds (2 wds.)
5 Canned meat
9 Big name in dental care (hyph.)
11 Sacred beetles
14 Mattress brand
15 Suit accessory
16 Remnant
17 Skinny
19 Bandleader Artie
20 __ Miguel
21 London art gallery
22 Compass pt.
23 When school starts again
25 "__ Gantry"
27 Commander
28 Beg
29 Seasonal songs
30 Plant bottom
31 "Baby __ Star" (Prince, 2 wds.)
32 Curl holder
34 "Now __ seen everything!"
37 Fiddling emperor
39 Hobbling
40 Corn ear
41 Enlists (2 wds.)
43 Brief forays
45 Irked
46 Pointed post
47 Sounds from guard dogs, perhaps
48 Put __ act (2 wds.)

DOWN

1 Firefighters' tools
2 Circular stadium
3 Having trouble with sound (3 wds.)
4 Flight height (abbr.)
5 Part of an act
6 __-Man (arcade game)
7 Places of refuge
8 Person who works with numbers
10 Military encounters
11 Little tantrum
12 Prejudiced
13 Embroiderer
18 Semi
24 Be unwell
25 They run off to wed
26 Sign of the Lion
27 Lure (hyph.)
28 Formally precise
29 "Teenage Mutant __ Turtles"
32 Crossword hints
33 Sgt. Joe Friday's employer (abbr.)
35 Bloody Mary ingredient
36 Buddy of "Barnaby Jones"
38 __ about (approximately, 2 wds.)
42 Israel's neighbor (abbr.)
44 From __ Z (2 wds.)

PUZZLE 16

ACROSS

1 Makes fit
7 Men's party
11 Order from Tony Soprano, e.g. (2 wds.)
12 Merry adventure
14 Google web browser
15 Raised the ante
16 Skeptic's comment (2 wds.)
17 Defrauds
18 Vinegary
21 Actor Andrews
22 Beachside cottage
24 Work __ sweat (2 wds.)
27 Alternative word
28 Individual
29 Cool drinks
30 It's the "racer's edge"
31 Serenity
33 Fuzzy "Return of the Jedi" character
36 "__ Bridge Is Falling Down"
37 Coffee type
39 Fisherman's need
40 Those against
41 "Who cares"
feeling
44 Filched
45 Ate hurriedly
46 Sources of metal
47 Haughty looks

DOWN

1 "Breaking Bad" network
2 Homer Simpson exclamation
3 Shorten by omissions
4 Strong fear
5 Where employees
punch in (2 wds.)
6 Proofreading comment
7 Underwater breathing apparatus
8 Short golf putt (2 wds.)
9 Commended
10 Weirdo
13 Streets (abbr.)
18 Vigoda et al.
19 Unorthodox religious group
20 Clouseau's title
21 Ponder moodily (2 wds.)
23 "Design __
Dime" (2 wds.)
25 Mexican moolah
26 Part of AARP (abbr.)
29 Actress Funicello
32 Group's mood
34 "Whistle __ You Work" (song)
35 Desert sites
37 Mothers
38 Aware of
39 Science rms.
42 "Take __, She's Mine"
43 Length measures (abbr.)

PUZZLE 17

ACROSS

1 "__ Come Undone" (Wally Lamb bestseller)
5 Shimmery mineral
9 Glittered
10 Platform
12 Merlot relative
13 The Silver State
15 Acorn products
16 Baby's wearable napkin
18 Sad sound
19 Mrs., in Paris
20 Knight's weapon
22 Modern (prefix)
23 African bird
25 "Rescue Me" star Denis
27 "The Hammer" of baseball (2 wds.)
29 "Get __!" ('90s dismissal, 2 wds.)
31 More flaxen-haired
34 Wine (Fr.)
35 Oft-printed newspaper
37 Wide street
38 Korbut of gymnastics
40 Classic racecar, for short
41 Week-ending inits.
42 Dale Jr.'s org.
44 Rafts
46 Opposite of bless
47 Callas of opera
48 __ Le Pew
49 __-steven

DOWN

1 Cause a ruckus (3 wds.)
2 __ d'oeuvres
3 Compass pt.
4 Snag in a plan
5 "Morning Joe" network
6 Finish for suburban or meteor
7 Nickname of Cleveland hoopsters
8 Repeatedly (3 wds.)
9 Bridge coups
11 Gardener's tool
12 "Hot Diggity" singer Perry
14 Sailor's cry
17 Dwell within
20 __ up (queued)
21 "The Jetsons" son
24 Battle of Britain gp.
26 Long period
28 #1 hit for John Legend (3 wds.)
29 English river
30 Spring flower
32 Musical set in Argentina
33 Foul callers, for short
36 Feel the same way
39 Development tract
41 Ripped
43 Venomous snake
45 Washroom, for short

ACROSS

1 Playground retort (2 wds.)
7 Ranked
12 Before deductions
13 In tune (2 wds.)
14 Where settlers got provisions (2 wds.)
16 Ocean liner (abbr.)
17 103, to Cato
18 Phrase akin to "I didn't do it!" (2 wds.)
20 Blockhead
24 Make blurry
27 Reaches a destination
29 Dosage units
30 Ryan of "Paper Moon"
31 Baffled (3 wds.)
34 Time-share unit, perhaps
35 Count (on)
36 Hikes
38 Restaurant reading
39 Sleeve card
42 Neil Simon comedy (3 wds.)
47 More than pleasantly plump
48 Filled with fear
49 Sheds skin
50 Talks impudently

DOWN

1 Fuel economy letters
2 Greek god
3 Clark __ (Superman)
4 Everlastingly
5 Spoil
6 On the button
7 More pink
8 Opposed
9 Boxing result (abbr.)
10 Always, to poets
11 Coloring
15 __ bean
19 Approximation phrase (2 wds.)
20 Prehistoric animals
21 Baking place
22 Expired
23 Norwegian capital
24 Sail support
25 Speck
26 Israeli airline (2 wds.)
28 Plymouth __
32 Stockholm residents
33 Beach particles
37 "Star Wars" creator George
38 Greatest amount
40 Accountants (abbr.)
41 Author Wiesel
42 Writer Clancy
43 "Watchmen" channel
44 Slithery swimmer
45 Birds __ feather... (2 wds.)
46 Magazine employees (abbr.)

PUZZLE 19

ACROSS

1 Epic story
5 "This __ sudden!" (2 wds.)
9 Trudges
12 Carpet ruiners
14 Actress Eden
15 First Greek letter
16 Frazier's rival
17 __-serve
19 Attention-getting sound
20 "My Name Is Asher __"
21 Trunk item (2 wds.)
23 TV talking horse (2 wds.)
25 River mouths
26 Heart test (abbr.)
29 Supplement
30 Fund drive
33 Stadium cheers
37 Examining thoroughly
40 Singer Peggy
41 __ squad
42 Presently
43 Negligent
44 Fails to include
46 Window hanging
48 Declines
49 Neville and Burr
50 Prospector's bonanza
51 "__ we forget"

DOWN

1 Less fresh, as bread
2 Reach
3 Chat
4 Gather
5 "Life __ cabaret, old chum..." (2 wds.)
6 Splash
7 Oscar winner Loren
8 "Do unto __ ..."
10 __ school
11 Light lunch
13 Consistent
14 Aromatic oil
18 Unfettered
22 Tundra creature
24 Used up
27 Sardine can attachment
28 Strip of con-tention
30 Vet's patient
31 Al of "Scar-face"
32 Darnell or Ronstadt
34 Gracie and Debbie
35 William Randolph __
36 Attractive
37 Declare openly
38 Asta's owner
39 Distort
45 Wind dir.
47 Author Edgar Allan __

PUZZLE 20

ACROSS

1 Workout spot for females (abbr.)
5 Tending toward (2 wds.)
10 Good cookie for dunking
11 Pals
14 Country singer Williams
15 Hits right to the third baseman (2 wds.)
17 Decides
18 Carter and Vanderbilt
19 Cal. neighbor
20 Tint
21 Proofreading comment
22 Pepsi, e.g.
23 Actress Winfrey
25 Watered down
27 Young bug
29 Ott or Brooks
30 Sandra Day __
34 Ohio tire city
38 "__ Lisa"
39 Mend argyles
41 Tavern drink
42 "__ my brother's keeper?" (2 wds.)
43 Brim
44 Alan of "Ray Donovan"
45 Puts to new uses
47 Rotisserie rod
48 Indignant outcry (2 wds.)
49 Biblical pronoun
50 Poorest
51 Partnership (abbr.)

DOWN

1 Pirate's shout (hyph.)
2 Cover in paper (2 wds.)
3 Basketball position
4 NASA approv-als (hyph.)
5 Musical key (hyph.)
6 Ready for anything
7 "A Christmas Carol" boy (2 wds.)
8 Golfers' pegs
9 Light switch positions
12 "__ pass Go..." (2 wds.)
13 Glove leather
16 What a DVR user might skip (2 wds.)
21 Knee-to-ankle bone
22 Be a sore loser
24 Tennis player Kournikova
26 Stand lazily
28 One learning to walk
30 Sharif or Bradley
31 Arrives
32 In the cooler (2 wds.)
33 Tempestuous ones
35 Kramden and Richardson
36 Golden __
37 Make tidy
40 Bowler's button
43 Reverberate
44 Nick and Nora's pooch
46 Evergreen shrub

PUZZLE 21

ACROSS

1 Splotch
5 Oklahoma city
10 Linney of "Ozark"
12 Lack-of-pep cause
14 Walk a beat
15 Recluses
16 Rescue worker (abbr.)
17 Out of control
19 Senior citizens' org.
20 When classes are in session
22 Charlotte of "The Facts of Life"
23 Toll roads (abbr.)
24 __ the hole (2 wds.)
26 Basketball tourney org.
28 Shakespeare, e.g.
29 Lame, as a joke
30 "Gone __"
32 Mauna __
33 Founder of Detroit
37 Ben & Jerry's competitor
39 Mocked
40 Not Rep. or Dem.
41 Astounds
43 Deputies
45 Social media pic, often
46 Flood protection
47 Remained uninvolved (2 wds.)
48 Blocker et al.

DOWN

1 Condemn
2 Foamy coffee
3 "Flags of __ Fathers"
4 NYC's theater street
5 Sermons
6 Numero __
7 Actress Olin
8 Mudslinger
9 __ siren (2 wds.)
11 Neutrogena competitor
13 Colorado resort town
14 Church seat
18 Yiddish sounds of dismay
21 Genghis __
24 Shortened, as a dictionary
25 Convoke
26 Pasta pieces
27 Crayon brand
29 Musical symbols
30 Interval
31 Just what's needed
33 Legendary engineer Jones
34 Tablecloth material
35 Pays to play
36 LPs' successors
38 Downy
42 Kid
44 Green or Mendes

ACROSS
1 Charged atoms
5 Parts of mittens
11 Ferber and Purviance
12 Nag about (2 wds.)
13 Crawled
14 Stopped from tipping over
16 Midway attraction
17 Make one yawn
18 Ball-propping gadget
19 GI's club
20 Do in
21 Catnap
22 "__ Snow" (2 wds.)
24 Acted silently
25 Insomniac's hope
26 Aquatic mammals
27 Overcharge for a ticket
28 Fad
29 Is mistaken
30 Provoke
31 Polite address
34 Cribbage term
35 Franklin and Bernanke
36 Q followers
37 Laboring
39 The Mamas and the __
40 Archie Bunker's little girl
41 Lithe
42 Escapes
43 Tour of __

DOWN
1 Elba of "The Wire"
2 Buck (3 wds.)
3 Neck region
4 Concorde's initials
5 Place to dab perfume
6 Like a tarantula
7 Egg (on)
8 Car's pace (abbr.)
9 Ravenous one's stomach, seemingly (2 wds.)
10 Goes "achoo!"
11 Beige's cousin
15 Legal paper
17 Radar image
20 Short stride
21 "Shrek" star Cameron
23 "Electric" swimmers
24 Fermented honey drink
25 Dickens's infamous piker
26 Married women in Madrid (abbr.)
27 Posted
28 Cuban line dances
30 He grants three wishes
32 Milan's land
33 Artifice
35 Swallow, e.g.
36 Spaghetti sauce brand
38 "Hello Mary __"
39 Mat

PUZZLE 23

ACROSS
1 Appoint
7 Hay bundle
11 Sportswear top, slangily
12 Transmitter
14 Nearly
15 Tooth-capping substance
16 Lowe and Reiner
17 "La Danse" painter Henri
18 Compass indication (abbr.)
19 "The Way of All __"
21 Unrevealed
23 Howl with laughter
27 Gravy __
28 Bea Arthur TV role
29 "Brian's __"
30 Faith
31 "It's been __ pleasure!" (2 wds.)
33 Cut awkwardly
35 Arranged to fit
39 Author John Dickson __
40 Athletic conference (2 wds.)
41 "__ for Sergeants"
(2 wds.)
43 Just __ (prepared one's phrase, 2 wds.)
44 Mobs
45 Mattel products
46 Defeated ones

DOWN
1 Take __ look at (2 wds.)
2 Leading musicians
3 Mexican headwear
4 Altar vows (2 wds.)
5 Enlistees, for short
6 Fish catcher
7 __ B'rith
8 Naval chiefs (abbr.)
9 Gymnast Suni et al.
10 __ Stanley Gardner
12 Aegean and Red
13 Captivate
17 Got together
19 Naval vessels
20 Spy novelist Deighton
22 Is able to
24 Parisian agreement
25 "Guys and Dolls" doll
26 Corruption foe
28 "Give __ break!" (2 wds.)
30 Slumber site
32 Descartes or Magritte
34 Printing machine
35 "This won't hurt __!" (2 wds.)
36 Fred Flintstone's pet
37 Government bureau (abbr.)
38 School gps.
39 Hubs (abbr.)
41 Flyers' gp.
42 Hugs on a card

PUZZLE 24

ACROSS

1 Pt. of speech
4 Back problem
8 College VIP
12 Mediterranean, e.g.
13 Channel marker
14 __ bean
15 What a nurse gives (abbr.)
16 Nonconforming
18 Manicotti filling
20 Hudson or Ford
21 Martini fruit
22 Shuts
24 Logical
25 Gentleman caller
26 Biblical king
28 Slackens speed
32 Honey-baked meats
34 "Tree of Life" actor
36 Tropical fruit
39 __ Lama
40 Evergreen tree
41 Calls (2 wds.)
43 Penance
45 Ottawa's prov.
46 Hair line
47 Falco of "Tommy"
48 Cpl. or sgt.
49 Corrida cheers
50 Finishes i's
51 "__ Loves Me"

DOWN

1 Houston baseballers
2 Samson's downfall
3 Inoculation fluid
4 "Take __ out of crime" (2 wds.)
5 Brusque
6 Ancient
author of "Odes"
7 "Peeper"
8 Doldrums
9 He created Eeyore
10 Bradley and Sharif
11 Actor Grant
17 Halloween spirit
19 Finished
23 Young woman
25 Cake with candles time (abbr.)
27 Midwest hub
29 October's
stone
30 Comedian Flip et al.
31 Sturdy
33 Managed (2 wds.)
35 Walk cautiously
36 Flower feature
37 Love dearly
38 Breathes rapidly
39 Escorts
40 Mob boss
42 Monogram unit (abbr.)
44 Between sm. and lg.

ACROSS

1 Brains, informally
7 Dairy farm baby
11 Police officer
12 "I Enjoy Being __" (2 wds.)
14 "__ of the Lambs"
15 Juliet's love
16 Apple Store purchase
17 Film critic Pauline
19 Spy's listening device
20 "...borrower __ a lender be"
21 Little kid
22 Pieces of turf
23 Cartoon from Japan
25 Dermatologist's concern
27 Biblical prophet
29 Squalls
33 Infant's bed
35 Sugary
36 Third letters
39 Cape Canaveral gp.
41 Side or late start
42 Physicians' org.
43 Real estate listing abbr.
44 Pet store purchase
45 Covered with lichen
47 Regain
49 Kick out
50 Romantic runaway
51 Tennis's Nastase
52 __ of London

DOWN

1 Footwear without laces (hyph.)
2 Disease with chills and fever
3 Inspired wonder
4 White House monogram
5 Tasteless
6 Untrustworthy sorts
7 Rob Reiner's dad
8 "Long, Long __"
9 Caribbean dance
10 Analyst Sigmund
13 Diaries
14 Biblical peak
18 Mouse-sighting sounds
21 Crying product
22 Winter flakes
24 Karaoke needs
26 "__ free country..." (2 wds.)
28 Female deer
30 Put new asphalt on
31 Business combinations
32 Pilot
34 Wooden keg
36 Attended
37 Texter's icon
38 Picasso's stand
40 Aroma
43 Computer unit
44 Xerox
46 Biology, e.g. (abbr.)
48 Pigeon murmur

PUZZLE 26

ACROSS

1 Piccolos' cousins
6 Walt Kelly comic
10 Parka
12 Teflon producer
14 "__ Weather"
15 Weaken
16 Media mogul Turner
17 Patty Berg's gp.
19 Wooden soldier, e.g.
20 Brandy glasses
23 Bogs
24 Gram or photo start
25 Most greasy
27 Brought into harmony
29 Hay fever inducer
32 "Champagne" bandleader
35 Aviation heroes
36 Interfering
39 Cold and slippery
40 Zippy
41 Actress __ West
42 Autocrat
44 Escarole
47 Incantations
48 Browns
49 Walked
50 Sheriff's force

DOWN

1 Observes Yom Kippur
2 Purpose
3 Gourmet
4 Make a mistake
5 Uncle with a beard and top hat
6 Cougar
7 Antonym (abbr.)
8 Beatnik's beard
9 Pizza topping
11 NASCAR's Petty
12 Starts a meal (2 wds.)
13 Meeting of lovers
18 More pleased with oneself
21 Defects
22 Head (Fr.)
23 Castro of Cuba
26 Indecent
28 Entices
29 Ransacks
30 Receive
31 Steam spewer
33 Boundaries
34 Scoundrels
37 Rit products
38 Silly birds
40 Retailed
43 Yasir Arafat's gp.
45 Brief sleep
46 Simon and Garfunkel, once

PUZZLE 27

ACROSS

1 Marine predator
5 Mind-bending drug (abbr.)
8 Sounds of doubt
11 Pursues ardently
12 Cool cubes
13 East Coast highway (2 wds.)
15 __ Hari
17 Muscular strength
18 Took a chance
20 Ann Landers, for one
22 Humane gp.
23 __-do-well
24 Dollywood's state (abbr.)
26 Porker's pad
27 Lariats
30 Want __
33 Where shares are traded (abbr.)
34 Docile
38 Rational
40 Unlawful
42 Dizzying sensation
44 Hibernation spots
45 Medicinal plant
46 Reason to take melatonin
48 Dutch __ disease
49 Actor Coleman
50 Laughing __
51 "Kidnapped" author's inits.
52 Reached base feetfirst

DOWN

1 1936 Olympics star Jesse
2 Kanga's baby
3 Like some political districts
4 On the Aegean
5 Tree branches
6 Resells for a big profit
7 Discover a clue
8 Citified
9 Multitude
10 Urbane
14 Spin a baton
16 An apple __... (2 wds.)
19 Lion feature
21 Handicrafts website
25 Seasonal song
28 "__ Love Her" (Beatles, 2 wds.)
29 Vapor
30 Edison's middle name
31 One settling a score with a weapon
32 Coiled document
35 Getting grayer
36 "Sound of Music" role
37 "Frozen" queen et al.
39 News paragraphs
41 Andrew __ Webber
43 Light carriages
47 __ Lanka

PUZZLE 28

ACROSS

1 HBO alternative
6 Vows
11 Marisa of "My Cousin Vinny"
12 Sound of brakes
15 Leek's cousin
16 TV angels' boss
17 Some NFL linemen (abbr.)
18 Kin of "arrivederci!"
20 "__ boy!"
21 Largest quantity
23 Gator's cousin
25 Pimple, to a teen
26 Malt brews
28 Runs away
30 Some German autos
32 Budweiser rival
33 Young ladies of Spain (abbr.)
34 Grate
35 Had breakfast
36 Tarzan's pals
38 Singer Cooke et al.
42 Cotton machines
44 Lupino and Tarbell
46 Sheep's sound
47 Jumped to conclusions
49 Tennis champion Chris
51 Utilize a wok (hyph.)
52 __ Meir
53 Rent contract
54 Poker phrase (hyph.)

DOWN

1 Tempest
2 Kemo Sabe's friend
3 Wrong
4 __ Speedwagon
5 Brass component
6 Actors' awards
7 Hay fever sufferer's sound
8 Refrain word
9 Wife of Zeus
10 Club soda's kin
13 Metropolises
14 Puts in the oven
19 Cools
22 Cry of accomplishment (hyph.)
24 Corporate money managers (abbr.)
27 Maggie Simpson's sis
29 Prunes, as branches
30 Museum exhibitor
31 Knife or fork
32 Hidalgo house
33 Narrative legends
34 What Lucille Ball used on her hair (2 wds.)
37 Docking places
39 "__ for Adano" (2 wds.)
40 __ Gras
41 Evil one
43 "No problem!"
45 Nintendo competitor
48 College deg.
50 Stereo knob (abbr.)

PUZZLE 29

ACROSS

1 Snow White's friends
7 "Andy __"
11 Veal __
12 Entreaty
13 Charm
14 Cassini of fashion
15 "A likely story!" (2 wds.)
16 __ wheel (VIP)
17 Mine find
18 Wide shoe width
19 Mare's baby
20 Arden and Plumb
21 Cut roughly
23 Dirty
25 Shad __
26 Respectful title
27 Boot part
30 Leave alone (2 wds.)
33 District in London
34 "The Women" playwright
36 Porkpie, for one
37 Tooth-pullers' org.
38 Airport abbr.
39 Thaw
40 Compact
42 Clear soup
44 Concludes
45 Shrove __
46 Collections
47 Filmdom's Meryl

DOWN

1 Famed racecar driver (2 wds.)
2 Formal document
3 Stubborn beast
4 2008 Stallone film
5 Threshes or thrashes
6 Wooed with a melody (2 wds.)
7 Naval noncom
8 Far and wide (4 wds.)
9 Looked at curiously
10 Bellboys
11 Actress Normand
13 Bonds
19 Atkins or Huntley
20 "Night" author Wiesel
22 Fair (hyph.)
24 Key
27 Red antiseptic
28 Votes in
29 Publish (2 wds.)
31 Like a summer breeze
32 Kitchen suffix
33 Money vaults
35 Chair seat maker
39 Method
41 Editors review them (abbr.)
43 Mariner's dir.

PUZZLE 30

ACROSS

1 Gent
5 "__ Sides Now"
9 Chubbier
12 Start of a magical phrase
13 Woman's lapel bouquet
14 __ Francis of Assisi
16 Med. school course
17 Second filming
18 "I __ Song Go..." (2 wds.)
19 151, Roman-style
21 "__ of the Mind" (2 wds.)
22 Soaking
25 Legislator (abbr.)
26 Estimated
28 Landing spot for milit. planes
31 Cartoon skunk (3 wds.)
35 Ocean mineral
37 Snake's sound
38 Big rig
39 Move quickly
41 Rate of walking
42 Mystical type of cards
43 Clothing
46 Jazzman Brubeck
47 Cooked steaks
48 Watches
49 Soothsayer

DOWN

1 Classic Ford
2 __ glance (2 wds.)
3 Limb
4 Prior, in poetry
5 Naval post
6 Only president born in Hawaii
7 Court cases
8 Tear dabber
9 Scorch
10 Photocopier liquid
11 Speak in public
15 High-schooler
17 Hoses off
19 Like most lasagna
20 Speaks imperfectly
23 Half a pint
24 Salon goop
27 Lose hope
28 Helper (abbr.)
29 False appearance
30 DVD's sophisticated relative (hyph.)
32 Oyster's creation
33 Quizmaster, e.g.
34 Control
36 Buried treasure
40 Map abbreviations
43 Stomach muscles, briefly
44 Season or historic start
45 "The Raven" poet

PUZZLE 31

ACROSS

1 "__ it!" (2 wds.)
5 Tabloid topics
9 Zenith
10 Peter in "Heidi," e.g.
15 Lend a hand
16 One "Great" (2 wds.)
17 Word's opposite
19 Beetle's tor-mentor
20 Performer Della
21 Actor Tim ("WKRP")
22 Subtract's opposite
23 Wild hog
27 Chances
28 __ to sleep (2 wds.)
30 Toothy game fish
33 Billiards
34 Flower visitor
37 Presently
38 Billy Joel's daughter __ Ray
40 Hook
42 Brings into the country
44 Put on the air
46 Like some antiques
47 Beginning
48 Relative of etc. (2 wds.)
49 Takes a load off
50 Loch __

DOWN

1 African desert
2 Unlocked
3 Sang strongly
4 Former Montreal team
5 Revolting
6 Insulation type
7 Hardwood tree
8 Holy Fr. females
11 Learn in passing (2 wds.)
12 Goofed
13 Inflexible
14 Accomplish-ments
18 Wyo. neighbor
24 "Alley __" (comic strip)
25 Letters in a soldier's address
26 Friend of Winnie-the-Pooh
28 Thicker
29 Wing movement
30 Agreements
31 Cove
32 Cute Aussie marsupial
34 Scold
35 Some cast members
36 Artists' tripods
39 Sophia of "Houseboat"
41 Army "grunts" (abbr.)
42 Doesn't exist
43 Actress Ryan et al.
45 Half of VI

PUZZLE 32

ACROSS

1 Eye covers
5 Small snakes
9 Reprobate
11 Jacob's wife
12 Tolerate
13 Greedily con-
   sumes(2 wds.)
15 Air
16 Issue forth
18 Citrus drink
19 "Hamlet" start
   (2 wds.)
21 Attention-
   getting sound
22 Dairy con-
   tainer (2 wds.)
25 Flowers
26 Language
30 Smart one's
   quality
32 Satie or Estrada
35 Diva Jenny
36 Congregated
37 Draws back
39 Respond to
   yeast
40 Starched
41 Starlet's role,
   perhaps
44 Umps' coun-
   terparts
45 Edible root
46 Approximation
   phrase
   (2 wds.)

47 Parker __
   (board game
   company)

DOWN

1 Barrymore et
   al.
2 "Trust __"
   ("Jungle
   Book" song,
   2 wds.)
3 Basis of
   heredity
   (abbr.)
4 Moment, infor-
   mally

5 "And to __
   good night!"
   (2 wds.)
6 "Milk" star
   (2 wds.)
7 Fathers
8 Closes
9 __ 54
10 Country star
   Thomas
12 Postage item
14 __ peeve
17 Glove's cousin
19 Cain and __
20 Howard of
   sportscasting
23 Bowl openers
24 Englishman's

title
27 Some born in
   June
28 Exhausts, as
   a resource
   (2 wds.)
29 Lauder of
   cosmetics
31 Drop by
32 Vocal pauses
33 Nostalgic style
34 More frosty
38 In that case
   (2 wds.)
39 Gambling city
42 Pencil stub
43 Rover's
   warning sound

PUZZLE 33

ACROSS

1 Goad (2 wds.)
6 Chops roughly
11 Place where a trial's held
12 Axis fighters in WWII
14 Love (Ital.)
15 Strew
17 Darkens
18 "This suitcase weighs __!" (2 wds.)
19 Former airport letters
20 Compass letters
21 "Good luck," to an actor (3 wds.)
23 Contempt
25 Prescriptions, informally
26 Choice words
27 Alphabetic trio
29 Loose cloak
32 New business venture
36 Eavesdropped
39 Spring mo.
40 Malarkey
41 "__ cost ya!"
42 Lifeguard's concern
43 Ferocious fish
45 Risotto relative
46 Determined
47 Greek vacation destination
48 Looks at rudely
49 Passover meal

DOWN

1 Eluded
2 Sign of the zodiac
3 Garden decorations
4 Not theirs
5 Born, in society pages
6 Hurry
7 Reynolds Wrap maker
8 Metallic sound
9 "__ Kittredge: An American Girl"
10 Arbitrate
13 Stitched
16 Riches' alternative
18 Onassis and namesakes
21 Taproom
22 Neighbor of Mexico (abbr.)
24 Accomplisher
27 Computer keyboard key
28 Pop
29 Inc. relative
30 Duck
31 Gasoline, in London
32 Leafy dishes
33 Followed
34 Software fix
35 "Gentlemen __ Blondes"
37 Pivot
38 Old-fashioned anesthetic
42 One of four on a car
44 Generation
45 Many computers (abbr.)

PUZZLE 34

ACROSS

1 Breathes heavily
6 Humiliate
11 Phrase on a Bumblebee can (2 wds.)
12 4 p.m. in London
14 Sandy Koufax, e.g.
15 Office file
16 Totals (abbr.)
17 Papal name
18 TX to NY dir.
19 Bro's female sib
20 Opposite of Amer., in baseball
21 Eliminates
22 American or Swiss
24 Marshes
25 Gabor and Peron
26 Desire
27 Miss a step
28 Respectable
30 Shopping spot
31 Bandleader Kyser et al.
32 NBC comedy sketch show
34 Doting attention (abbr.)
35 Newsstand offerings, briefly
36 One opposed
37 Foster
39 "Nutcracker" girl
40 Equine shelters
41 Speedy horse
42 "Barnaby Jones" star
43 Startled shout

DOWN

1 Venomous desert dwellers
2 Lacking iron
3 Seafood favorite (2 wds., hyph.)
4 Peach centers
5 Furtive
6 South Korean capital
7 Holbrook and others
8 From __ Z (2 wds.)
9 PM craving (2 wds.)
10 Corrects
12 Clichéd
13 Former spouses
17 Sentry's reply
20 Tide type
21 Betsy or Diana
23 Corrupt
24 Slant
26 Reasons
27 Greet the general
28 Batting __
29 Dinner course
30 Alps, e.g. (abbr.)
31 Actress Valentine
33 Untruthful ones
35 Stubborn beast
36 Jai __
38 Recipe measure (abbr.)
39 Shed tears

PUZZLE 35

ACROSS

1 Spies (abbr.)
5 Washed out suds
11 Rug's location
12 Convert into secret writing
13 Parts played
14 Elephants' treats
16 No ifs, __, or buts
17 Boxer Max
18 Co.'s head
19 Golf prop
20 Dry
21 Apple products
22 More agreeable
24 "Something's __ Give"
25 Norwegian inlet
26 Ponchos
27 Terre __
28 Propelled a dinghy
29 "Fantastic Four" actress Jessica
30 Eccentric person
31 Auto owner's expense
34 Ted Danson TV show
35 Short haircuts
36 "It's __ a shame!"
37 '60s TV doctor
39 Composition
40 Antenna
41 Facial features
42 Raise one's voice toward (2 wds.)
43 Throw lightly

DOWN

1 Solo
2 Special anniversary (2 wds.)
3 Stubbing victims
4 Last-year students (abbr.)
5 Fix
6 "__ You" (Beatles song, 2 wds.)
7 Duke's st.
8 Junior, to Dad
9 Estimate, perhaps (2 wds.)
10 Discovers
11 Campus gp.
15 "Slamming Sammy"
17 Raised, as animals
20 Farm division
21 Become listless
23 Small quantity
24 Stare stupidly
25 Make fake
26 Pigeons' cries
27 Writer for hire
28 Actor Ryan
30 "M*A*S*H" setting
32 Highest points
33 "__ Leaving Home"
35 Society dance
36 "Scat!"
38 Singer Shannon
39 Blasting letters

PUZZLE 36

ACROSS

1 Inexpensive
6 Shut noisily
10 Total Car Care chain
11 Cowboy's "nightclub"
14 Solid piece, as of marble
15 "__ Else But Me"
16 Stung
18 "If You Knew __"
19 Eatery
20 Watch-chain ornament
22 Athletic event
23 Tom Watson's gp.
24 Soft quilts
26 Tyrannosaurus __
27 Connect
28 __ a plea
31 Latin dance
32 Air hero
33 Very top
36 __ Aviv
37 Kitchen equipment
38 Best part
40 Soap opera, e.g.
42 Revoke
44 "__, Young Lovers"
45 Dances to Big Band jazz
46 Film critic Roger
47 Conclude
48 Pickford and Poppins

DOWN

1 Sauerkraut ingredient
2 Nova Scotia's capital
3 Show a lot of feeling
4 Part of CPA
(abbr.)
5 Tease (3 wds.)
6 Taxpayer's ID
7 Cambodia's neighbor
8 Musician's output
9 Deer's relative
12 Garfield's canine pal
13 No, to a Russian
17 Rookies
19 Lifesaving technique (abbr.)
21 "O Little Town of __"
24 "No fooling!"
25 Brit's afternoon beverage
28 Troops on horseback
29 Leopardlike animals
30 Hutch
31 Glue firmly
33 Tax mos.
34 Work gang
35 Short skirts, for short
37 Greaser
39 Word on a waffle box
41 McEntire of country
43 Predictor's claim (abbr.)

PUZZLE 37

ACROSS

1 Amiss
5 Case or way preceder
10 Flop
12 Ends of rivers
14 "__ mind?" (2 wds.)
15 Systemized
17 List shortener (abbr.)
18 Mattress brand
20 Goat's bleat
21 Grade an egghead never gets
22 Enmity
23 German gentleman
24 __-daisy
25 Air __ (military branch)
26 Spooky
28 Severe
29 "Back in the Saddle __"
30 Wahine's dance
31 Preston and Bilko (abbr.)
32 Winter pear
33 Some ER cases
36 Business collaborative (abbr.)
37 Car insurance spokescritter
38 "Alias" gp.
39 Virginia town
41 "Chicago Med" network (2 wds.)
43 Barney of the comics
44 Fry quickly
45 Courted
46 AL MVP in 2007 (hyph.)

DOWN

1 Tacked on
2 Composed a letter
3 Rolls-__
4 "__-hoo!" (attention-getting call)
5 __ pants
6 Rich dessert
7 Mystical glow
8 Give __ whirl (2 wds.)
9 Poets, often
11 Tack's cousin
13 Seek
16 Risk
19 Relaxed state
23 Israeli dance
24 Writer Leon
25 Hawks' kin
26 Christmas party quaff
27 Be humiliated (2 wds.)
28 Shuck
29 Z __ zebra (2 wds.)
30 Used a pawn shop
32 Ball beauty
33 Happen
34 "Me, too!"
35 Rescued
37 __ boots (hyph.)
40 Rock's Fighters
42 Ewe's comment

PUZZLE 38

ACROSS

1 Vittles
5 Swift river currents
11 Take game illegally
12 Pierre's emphatic affirmative (2 wds.)
13 Paperboy's course
14 Made coffee
15 Fully prepared (2 wds.)
17 Remove entirely
18 Storage spot
19 Pt. of speech
21 Nabisco sandwich cookies
24 Bush and Washington
29 Table setting items
31 Motion pictures
32 Polite affirmative (2 wds.)
34 Merits
35 Mauna __
36 Switch positions
37 Mirror reflection
41 "I __ be so lucky!"
45 Experience again in the imagination
47 Start of a famous series
48 Goes upward
49 Laid bathroom floor
50 Prickly plant
51 Chief actor

DOWN

1 Indifference
2 Tote
3 Birth months for some Libras (abbr.)
4 Exuberant cry
5 Pilfer
6 So long, in Soissons (2 wds.)
7 Fishing spot
8 Minnesota's neighbor
9 Union payment
10 Agree (with)
11 "Little House on the __"
16 Merchandise dangler
18 Torso
20 Christmas's mo.
22 Electrical unit
23 Elevation reference point (2 wds.)
25 Genetic inheritance letters
26 Age (2 wds.)
27 Made corrections
28 Show cheeky insolence
30 __ Paulo, Brazil
33 Barker and Kettle
37 Formerly Persia
38 Trifle description
39 Dismounted
40 Pith
42 Sombreros, e.g.
43 Passing notice, informally
44 Home of the Bruins (abbr.)
46 Compass letters

PUZZLE 39

ACROSS

1 Conway and Allen
5 Without __ in the world (2 wds.)
10 Highway access (hyph.)
13 Bamboozled
14 Making sense
15 Divisions at Macy's (abbr.)
16 Graceful trees
17 Piglets' mamas
19 Little white __
20 Drivers' org.
21 Hollywood's Preminger
22 Banana discard
23 Hat material
25 Dog's nose
27 __ National (hot dog brand)
29 Brown songbird
32 "The Greatest Showman" actor Zac
34 Left Bank "thanks"
35 Sun. speeches
37 Paddy product
39 Beatty or Rorem
40 Math course (abbr.)
41 Dropped down
42 Excellent (2 wds.)
43 "The Lion King" lion
45 Develops with care
47 Stable division
48 Polite tea drinker
49 Yiddish gossip
50 Whig's foe

DOWN

1 Past the deadline (2 wds.)
2 "Scenes from a Marriage" director (2 wds.)
3 Diagnosis tools (abbr.)
4 Cul-de-__
5 Does sums
6 Stage signal
7 Fruity dessert (2 wds.)
8 Fasten again
9 Ford lemon
11 Crow's-nest pole
12 Plans
14 Dog walker's need
18 "__ you be my neighbor?" (Mr. Rogers)
21 Debtor
22 Untainted
24 Sounds of barking
26 Words of worry (2 wds.)
28 Was dressed in
30 Picturesque view
31 Skins
33 Frasier Crane's brother
35 Bold
36 Privileged group
38 Roman 156
41 Refrain sounds (2 wds.)
42 Purina competitor
44 Deli sandwich letters
46 Select

PUZZLE 40

ACROSS
1 Kind of steak (hyph.)
6 Sandbox toys
11 Luxurious pelts
12 Admit (2 wds.)
13 Boring tools
14 Store that sells chew toys
15 Large African antelope
16 Pastrami parlor
18 "I __ Ike"
20 __ time (never, 2 wds.)
22 1492 ship
24 Judge's expertise
25 Filled tortilla
27 Eeyore's creator
29 Designer of bridges (2 wds.)
33 Ascend
34 Vessel
35 Home (abbr.)
36 Santa __, California
38 Neuter
42 Roman 552
44 Sanction
46 Historic time
47 Storage spot
49 __ T. Washington (educator)
51 "I'll never grow up, __"
("Peter Pan," 2 wds.)
52 Given, but expected to be returned (2 wds.)
53 Reduces, as speed
54 Flanks

DOWN
1 Jeer at
2 Country kid's weapon (2 wds.)
3 Spanish arena cheer
4 Mr. Cool's opposite
5 Central part
6 Visit for a bit (2 wds.)
7 Reverence
8 Worldwide (abbr.)
9 Little Richard hit
10 Washington locale
11 Norse legend
17 Disney's Simba, initially (2 wds.)
19 Oversized pitcher
21 "Miss __ Regrets"
23 French friends
26 Actor Guinness
28 Calligrapher's needs
29 Postal __
30 Dublin's country
31 Social caller
32 Park structures
37 Runs competitively
39 Tea type
40 Vicinities
41 Knitting necessity
43 "Tell __ the judge" (2 wds.)
45 Singer Braxton
48 Mischief-maker
50 "This __ House"

PUZZLE 41

ACROSS
1 Upper body
6 "Saturday Night Fever" music
11 Boston basketball player
12 Writer Poe's middle name
13 Avow
14 Plain-spoken
15 Pub order
16 Alone
18 Nibble on
20 "Peter Pan" pooch
22 Predicament
24 Bobby of hockey
25 Cut calories
27 Connecticut Ivy Leaguer
29 Close kin (2 wds.)
33 Lather, ___, repeat
34 Rave
35 Just get by
36 False
38 Chihuahua's comments
42 Saturates
44 First grader's school (abbr.)
46 '30s relief agency (abbr.)
47 Certain relative
49 Just around the corner (2 wds.)
51 Computer message
52 Severe upset
53 Lunch spots
54 Dazes

DOWN
1 Electric auto
2 Mary-Kate or Ashley
3 Map abbr.
4 "Camelot" titles
5 Tenth month
6 Apply, as perfume (2 wds.)
7 "Well, ___ be!"
8 Snail's relative
9 Trattoria dessert
10 Canadian province
11 "Godfather" actor James
17 Reproduced word for word
19 Small bird
21 Commotions
23 Cannon of "Ally McBeal"
26 March date
28 Lawyer (abbr.)
29 Make beer
30 Compared
31 ___ offer (hyph.)
32 Bewails
37 Scoundrels
39 Not to be taken seriously (2 wds.)
40 Baby carriages
41 ___ Ramirez of "Grey's Anatomy"
43 Performing mammal
45 Cartoonist Walker
48 102 in Old Rome
50 It follows sigma

PUZZLE 42

ACROSS

1 Gaza or Sunset
6 Large bag
10 Valentine's shape
11 Sequence of words
13 Bars on cars
14 Edible crustacean
16 Brisk knock
17 Prepares hides
18 Gob's reply
19 Breathing in
22 Pack freight
23 Where life begins
24 Present
25 Injury
28 Got more mileage from
29 "__ Ike" (2 wds.)
30 "Sister Act" roles
31 "Or __!"
32 Flashy showoffs
36 Songwriter Kahn
37 Ruin a hairdo
38 Pursue ardently
39 Japanese folding art
41 Decaf brand
43 Magic potion
44 Ewes, e.g.
45 Blyton or Bagnold
46 Puts on guard

DOWN

1 Actress Belafonte
2 Dallas native
3 Consumer advocate Nader
4 Great wrath
5 Two make a qt.
6 Bikini type
7 Spheres
8 Professors' helpers (abbr.)
9 Haciendas
11 Alternative course of action (2 wds.)
12 Donkey in Milne books
15 Void the divorce
17 Clock information
20 Facing the day
21 Theater box
22 "Quiet!"
24 Perfect ratings
25 San __ Padres
26 Fascination
27 Scud or ICBM, for example
28 Road indentations
30 Polite refusal (2 wds.)
32 Full of moisture
33 Name on the deed
34 "A __ of my esteem"
35 Detergents
37 Skirt style
40 Popular liquor
41 Compass pt.
42 "Gotcha!"

PUZZLE 43

ACROSS

1 Dutch shoe
5 Munich car co.
8 Very uncommon
9 Govern
10 LP alternatives
13 Has anted (2 wds.)
14 Building extensions
15 Regal letters
16 Ship's cheapest accommodation
18 Roman 53
19 Type of TV cabinet
20 Soothing influence
21 Frequently, in verse
22 Broke up an organization
24 Nickname for Margaret
25 Haul
26 Eli Whitney invention (2 wds.)
30 Dentist's degree (abbr.)
33 Destroys
34 Following a food plan (3 wds.)
36 Features at many banks (abbr.)
37 Invites (2 wds.)
38 Caesar's 1,501
39 Deceive
40 Mature
41 Seed holder
42 TV's talking horse (2 wds.)
43 Already learned
44 Kilmer of "The Saint"
45 Sunday talks (abbr.)

DOWN

1 Alternative to lard
2 "The __ the Mohicans" (2 wds.)
3 Use a compass
4 Heredity factors
5 Protrusions
6 Parisian female (abbr.)
7 NBA's Unseld
9 Straighten again
10 Chef Julia
11 Hit a golf ball
12 Started suddenly
17 Bronco-riding events
18 "Metropolis" director Fritz
20 Sweatboxes
23 Looked with surprise
24 Peaks (abbr.)
26 __ one's style
27 Excel
28 Like a rabbit
29 Apostles' teaching
30 "__ Comedy"
31 More profound
32 Scatters
35 Nerds' kin
37 Subtle atmosphere
39 Would-be driver's destination (abbr.)

PUZZLE 44

ACROSS

1 Gold-loving monarch
6 Norman Vincent __
11 "Old MacDonald had __" (2 wds.)
12 Felt
13 Piebald horse
14 Gasoline additive
15 AFL-__
16 Nag about (2 wds.)
17 Hearty Italian soup
21 Slippery __
22 "We __ People..."
23 Denominations
27 Grandstand part
29 __ and Marty Krofft (TV producers)
31 Horse father
32 Female and male
34 U.S. soldiers
36 Be unwell
37 Impervious to noise
40 Little green men
43 __ kwon do (martial art)
44 Memorizes
45 "Luther" star Elba
48 Colorado city
49 Signified
50 Valuable thing
51 Ferber and others

DOWN

1 Motorist's aid
2 "__ Had a Hammer" (2 wds.)
3 Waltz or hustle
4 Painter
5 Uses a sander on
6 Georgia crop
7 Dinner courses
8 PDQ's kin
9 Fallon's preceder
10 Adam's garden
12 NYC neighborhood
17 '69 World Series stars
18 Tennis star Nastase
19 Taos's state (2 wds., abbr.)
20 Royal rule
24 Pretentious sort's "bye-bye"
25 Singing group
26 __-service
28 Book in advance
30 Went to jail (2 wds.)
33 Short poem
35 Turned earth in a garden
38 Cold War inits.
39 Showed again
40 He played Pierce on "M*A*S*H"
41 Grant and Marvin
42 Ziering and Fleming
46 __ pickle (2 wds.)
47 Easy and Main (abbr.)

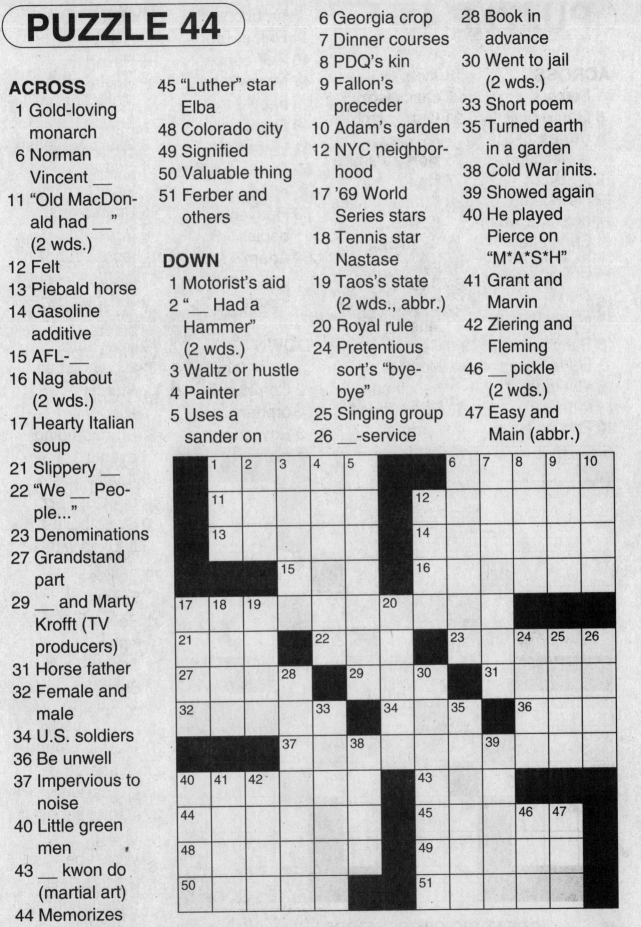

PUZZLE 45

ACROSS

1 Lethal
6 Garbo of film
11 Professor's protection
12 __ blue
13 Newspaper notice (2 wds.)
14 Early afternoon hour (2 wds., abbr.)
15 "__ Lay Dying" (2 wds.)
16 Baby's after-bottle sound
18 Thailand, formerly
20 End for lob or mob
22 Quick look
24 Out __ limb (2 wds.)
25 Horse's snack
27 Clergyman
29 What a tie ties (2 wds.)
33 "Lou Grant" actor
34 "Mona __"
35 Speedometer letters
36 Captain Hook's henchman
38 Bed support
42 Burpee product ·
44 Helper (abbr.)
46 Self-concept
47 Move like a baby
49 Fur for a king
51 __ basin
52 Carried with effort
53 Heavenly bodies
54 Adam's son and namesakes

DOWN

1 __ or famine
2 Comic strip orphan
3 Egyptian boy-king
4 Syrian, e.g.
5 Paved the way for (3 wds.)
6 Fumble
7 "This Is Us" actor __ Cephas Jones
8 Needle holes
9 Kind of pudding
10 Reference book
11 "__ the night before..."
17 Thrift store transactions
19 Gospel book
21 Part
23 Soldiers of the lowest rank (abbr.)
26 LAX postings
28 Some nest eggs (abbr.)
29 Collides
30 Facets
31 Receive as a legacy
32 Some trucks
37 Shopping complexes
39 Vivien or Janet
40 Actress Moorehead
41 Pigeon-__
43 Baby word
45 Undistorted
48 Civil __
50 The opposite of labor (abbr.)

ACROSS

1 Cable choice (abbr.)
5 Blind as __ (2 wds.)
9 Bar mitzvah dance
10 1996 Presidential candidate
11 It's the "racer's edge"
14 Tennis's Lendl
15 Orchestra instrument
16 Double this for a dance
17 Fairway chunk
19 Double-crosses
21 Thrift
23 Hurts
24 __ Plaines
25 Eyeglass lens holders
27 "...was blind but now __" (2 wds.)
28 Man on a penny
30 Lhasa __
33 Doubtful
34 City dweller's bldg.
37 Ryan or Cara
39 Otalgia
41 Related
43 "Rocket Man" singer John
44 Island garland
45 Tan, in fashion
47 A Sinatra
48 Lisper's problem letter
49 Cut short
50 Uniform
51 Casserole ingredient
52 Recline

DOWN

1 Reproved
2 Nunnery's newcomer
3 Audience cheers
4 Church law
5 Bustle
6 "Don't Worry, Be Happy" guy (2 wds.)
7 Sunburn-healing plant
8 Fangs
11 Battle mementos
12 Cooking herb
13 Out of style
18 Actress Spelling
20 Drizzle
22 Knee-exposing skirt
26 Lounge
28 Actress Anderson
29 Ancient stringed instrument
30 Airplane seat choice
31 Uses a crowbar
32 Big rigs
34 Lively
35 Rings up
36 Inhabitant
38 Vote in
40 Change
42 Bill of Rights defenders (abbr.)
46 __ creek (2 wds.)

PUZZLE 47

ACROSS

1 Cries of surprise
5 Prague native
10 Wrangler rivals
12 Skin eruptions
14 Most gentle
15 Fund drive
16 Healers' group (abbr.)
17 Race tipster
19 Actress Campbell
20 Concentrate
22 Remove
23 Mined minerals
24 Celestial regions
26 Sagan or Reiner
28 Peaty wasteland
29 Orderly grouping
30 Unkempt person
32 Digit (abbr.)
33 Thin, high heel
37 Broadway light
39 Domain
40 Toddler's question
41 Keys or Silverstone
43 Small item
45 Disciplined
46 Alan of "Argo"
47 Votes in favor
48 Lullaby

DOWN

1 San Antonio landmark
2 Macho guy (hyph.)
3 Broad street (abbr.)
4 Loving
5 Wooden case
6 Use a microwave, informally
7 "NFL Live" network
8 British "bye-bye"
9 Harder to carry
11 Large pebble
13 Arctic vehicles
14 Tic-___-toe
18 Abbr. on a navy vessel
21 Explorer of TV
24 Burns slowly
25 NBA legend Bryant
26 The "C" in A.S.P.C.A.
27 Large wardrobe
29 Karenina and Christie
30 Bus depot (abbr.)
31 Cardellini or Evans
33 Narrow boards
34 Country music's Shania
35 "A Funny ___ Happened..."
36 Popeye's Olive
38 Military detective show
42 Solid water
44 Boxing term (abbr.)

PUZZLE 48

ACROSS

1 Tomato plant holder-upper
6 Some pre-college exams (abbr.)
11 "It's been __ pleasure!" (2 wds.)
12 "The Blue __"
14 Goes on a cruise
15 Tailor, at times
17 Insurance option (abbr.)
18 Certain appliances
19 Third letter
20 Chased
23 Some high-school diplomas (abbr.)
24 Electrical units
25 Uncle Miltie
26 Smack
29 "I have __ begun to fight" (2 wds.)
30 "21" singer
31 Beaut
32 Insect eggs
33 Scout's spike (2 wds.)
36 Outlawed pesticide (abbr.)
37 Females
38 Contend
40 More pert
42 "My Fair Lady" role
44 Nova __
45 Sewed joints
46 Try hard
47 Paddler's boat

DOWN

1 Beauty queen's identification
2 Vagabond
3 Letters sold by Pat Sajak
4 Penn of "Designated Survivor"
5 Raised railways
6 Spots
7 Dieter's meal
8 Insurance sellers (abbr.)
9 Sock part
10 Witchcraft
13 Seattle's Space __
16 Adjust again
18 __ roast
21 Tosses dice
22 Clog or loafer
23 Arise (2 wds.)
25 Locking device
26 Magicians' rods
27 Reebok competitor
28 Romaine or redleaf
29 "Sister Act" sisters
31 Observe with wicked intent (2 wds.)
33 "__ Finest Hour"
34 Aquafina alternative
35 Doodad
37 Locale
39 Relaxation
41 Wally of "Mr. Peepers"
42 Computer's exit key
43 Actress Michele

PUZZLE 49

ACROSS

1 Actress Irene
5 Featuring __ of thousands (2 wds.)
10 __ with a kiss
12 Rae played by Sally Field
13 Grow bigger
14 Arose (2 wds.)
15 Confronts
16 Registers
17 Have some soda
18 London's Big __
19 Guitar master
___ Paul
20 Mater lead-in
23 Deride
27 Follower (suffix)
28 "Teenage Mutant ___ Turtles"
30 Midwest state (abbr.)
31 Ocean bottoms
33 Mare's off-spring
34 Starz rival, for short
35 Bankbook abbr.
37 Labor __
39 The quietest Marx
42 In a shy way
44 Bungling
45 Arranged in order
46 Cavalry sword
47 "Could be" (2 wds.)
48 Fixed look
49 Playwright Hart

DOWN

1 Kind of chicken
2 Sitka citizen
3 Lease
4 Tallies
5 Corner formation
6 Sounding like a lovebird
7 Bachelor of __
8 Particle of soot
9 Raps gently
10 Conceal
11 Cut out, as a text passage
15 Talk off-the-cuff (hyph.)
18 __ California (Mexican peninsula)
21 Elevate
22 P preceders
24 Interior parts
25 Views
26 Dark wood
29 College graduate
32 Straw user
36 "The Hunch-back of __ Dame"
38 Sneakers advertised by Jordan
39 Snaky sound
40 Medical school course (abbr.)
41 McEntire of country
42 Minor haircut
43 "Othello" bad guy

PUZZLE 50

ACROSS

1 Univ. student's home, perhaps
5 Army NCOs
9 Busy as ___ (2 wds.)
10 Earring type
11 Pacino et al.
14 Southern pronoun
15 Fringe
16 52, to Caesar
17 Singer Kate ___
19 Deducting from wages
21 Corridor
23 Deadly Sins number
24 Soot
25 Valentine's Day gift
27 Cravings
28 Pinata parties
30 Land parcel
33 Washing compound
34 Texter's "wow!"
37 Winter weather
39 Famous TV dolphin
41 Gardener's purchase
43 Davis of "Hero"
44 Yoko ___
45 Unknown author (abbr.)
47 Connecting words
48 Stop working (abbr.)
49 Prima donna
50 Percolate
51 Proofreading instruction
52 Makes mistakes

DOWN

1 Pedicure place (2 wds.)
2 Former White House family
3 Frankfurter topping
4 Thaws
5 Ship's pronoun
6 Venus (3 wds.)
7 Fast-food directive (2 wds.)
8 Glasses, for short
11 "We've got ___ one!" (2 wds.)
12 Flax product
13 Indicators
18 Spy Mata ___
20 They open doors
22 "As Time ___ By"
26 Footnote abbr. (2 wds.)
28 Professional charges
29 Sweat like ___ (2 wds.)
30 Actress Mary
31 Genetic copy
32 Transplant a fern
34 First game of the season
35 Seamstress, at times
36 Understands
38 Adult tadpoles
40 "___ Porridge Hot"
42 Monogram pt.
46 D.C. baseballer

PUZZLE 51

ACROSS

1 Innocent ones
6 Slide over
10 1996 Madonna film
11 __ Fireball (cinnamon candy)
13 Belle's speech feature
14 "The Godfather" director
16 Conway or Russert
17 DiCaprio et al.
18 Can material
19 Italian export (2 wds.)
22 "__ you be my neighbor?" (Mr. Rogers)
23 Mary Kay rival
24 Gulps down
25 Store at many malls (2 wds.)
28 Elegantly stylish
29 Broadcast again
30 Shoe filler
31 Besides that
32 St. Louis baseballer
36 Comic strip scream
37 Retirees' org.
38 Yale student
39 Cold-sufferer's sound
41 Actress Day
43 Certain mollusks
44 White Russian ingredient
45 Place or James
46 Prescribed portions

DOWN

1 Resulted in (2 wds.)
2 Pop punk singer Lavigne
3 "Golden Girls" setting
4 Incidentally, to a texter
5 Mineo of "Exodus"
6 Backless chair
7 Prunes, as branches
8 Ref's counterpart
9 Boisterous
11 __ the hole (2 wds.)
12 Adheres
15 Raring to go
17 Pilot's stunt
20 Not clearly expressed
21 Actress __ Rachel Wood
22 "That's __ was afraid of!" (2 wds.)
24 Lump of clay
25 Orchard members
26 Mount St. __
27 Writer Caldwell
28 Inc. relative
30 Passengers
32 __ spade a spade (2 wds.)
33 Dweebs
34 Showing a strong resemblance
35 Simpson and Hartman
37 Throw __ (flip out, 2 wds.)
40 Portly
41 Thing that Netflix used to send
42 Goose eggs

PUZZLE 52

ACROSS

1 __ plexus
6 Dairy sounds
10 Colored line
11 Gush
12 Hawthorne's "The __ Letter"
13 Nimble
14 Above, to poets
15 Drag the bottom for fish
17 Footballer Namath
18 "Lamp __ My Feet"
20 Dublin's country
22 Window part
23 "What's in __?" (2 wds.)
24 Did perfectly
25 Seed
26 "__ Girl"
30 Merits
32 Mangle
33 Bash
36 They cover Highland heads
37 Fabray, to friends
38 Legendary quarterback John
41 Letter after sigma
42 Honest __ day is long (2 wds.)
44 Pie __ (3 wds.)
46 Kitchen device
47 Reduces
48 Granny, for one
49 Pulmonary pair

DOWN

1 Take by surprise
2 Bobby of hockey
3 Swingy tune
4 Mimicker
5 It holds back soil (2 wds.)
6 Auto ad abbr.
7 Séance message board
8 Man-made fabric
9 Cavalryman's mount
10 Eye-pleasing
11 "Days of Our Lives" town
12 March man
16 Envelops
19 Ancient
21 Within the law, for short
23 "__ Showers"
27 Eloquent speakers
28 Wanderers
29 Follow
31 "Doe, __..." (2 wds.)
33 Light meal
34 Is dressed in (2 wds.)
35 Opening remarks
39 Outfielder Matty
40 Act bored
43 __ up (excited)
45 Actress Tilly et al.

PUZZLE 53

ACROSS

1 Zoo dweller
7 Kaplan who played Kotter
11 Secondhand transaction
12 Rang bells
14 "Sex and the City" lead
15 Oktoberfest orders
16 Blocking from view
18 Lave
21 __ Palmas
22 Largest continent
23 Russo of "Big Trouble"
24 __ Lanka
27 Very toned (hyph.)
30 Map marking (abbr.)
31 "Born Under __ Sign" (2 wds.)
32 Trot
33 Done with working (abbr.)
34 Locates
35 Ivy League college in NJ
39 Sarcastic
40 Van Gogh flowers
44 Celica maker
45 Conceited one
46 Part of AARP (abbr.)
47 One of Santa's reindeer

DOWN

1 __ de Triomphe
2 Teacher's gp.
3 Tel Aviv location (abbr.)
4 Law officer
5 Wonderland visitor
6 Stare at rudely
7 Leslie Caron title role
8 Prayer ending
9 Floating chunk of ice
10 Author McBain et al.
12 Removed dirt from
13 __ and Gretel
17 Exalt
18 Whine
19 Not in port
20 __-a-Whirl
23 Du Maurier classic
24 Extend over
25 Shipping dept. stamp
26 The __ of March
28 "Oh, man!" (2 wds.)
29 Viewpoint
34 Renounce
35 Paid athletes
36 Orbison et al.
37 __ the ground floor (2 wds.)
38 Fastened
39 "Isn't __ Pity" (George Harrison, 2 wds.)
41 Moral wrong
42 Wind dir.
43 Ocean craft (abbr.)

PUZZLE 54

ACROSS
1 Poetic verses
5 Mail __
10 Merry tunes
12 Led to a seat
14 Assign a portion
15 Clemens and Morse
16 Fireplace sight
17 Justice __ Kagan
18 Chile's neighbor
20 Naughty children
23 Peanut butter brand
26 Dads
28 Lubricates
29 Join the military
31 Isn't able to
33 Read hastily
34 Puncture
36 Certain doctors (abbr.)
37 Kind
38 Killer whale
40 Artist Picasso
43 Friend of Pythias
47 Forsake
49 Writer Jong
50 Negative statements
51 Two score
52 Rocky wharf
53 Capone's enemy

DOWN
1 "Frozen" snowman
2 Pickling herb
3 Jazz great Fitzgerald
4 Dance at the Savoy
5 Words of worry (2 wds.)
6 Alumni get-together
7 Imagining
8 Slippery
swimmer
9 Streets (abbr.)
11 Soaks
12 Exhaust (2 wds.)
13 Bando or Maglie
19 Decomposes
21 Fall heavily
22 Some jets (abbr.)
23 Banter
24 Covered with writing fluid
25 Irreverent
27 Wound remainder
30 Words of warning (3 wds.)
32 Alphabetic sequence
35 Characters in "Who Framed Roger Rabbit"
39 "Breaking Bad" actor Paul
41 Reason for cake, informally
42 Online chuckle
44 Marsh
45 Birth months for some Libras (abbr.)
46 "No" votes
47 Word like "pretty" (abbr.)
48 Busy as a __

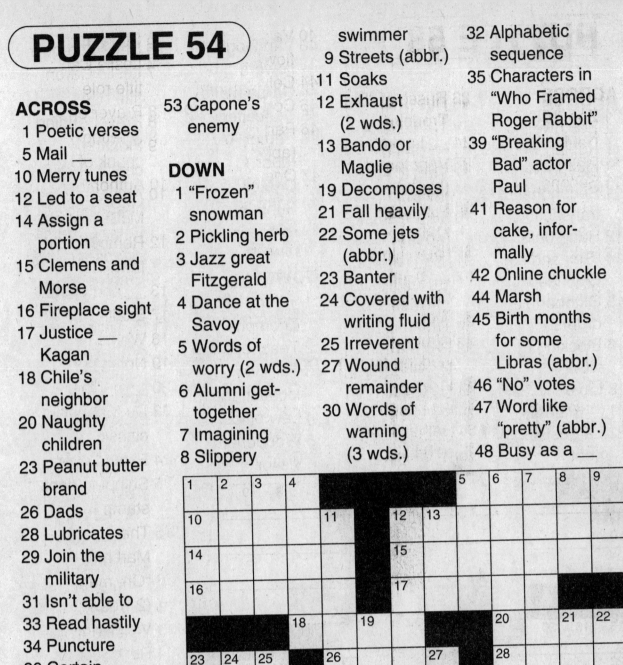

PUZZLE 55

ACROSS
1 Garland
7 Detroit's st.
11 Head and Shoulders, e.g.
12 Certain hairdo
13 Rainbow's band of colors
14 Couple
15 Add to the staff
16 Money set aside for later years (abbr.)
17 Mind-bending drug (abbr.)
18 Raw rock
19 Give __ up (help, 2 wds.)
20 Ballet move
21 Mails
23 Invoices
25 Cycle prefix
26 USN rank
27 Drink after hard liquor
30 Supply station
33 School for first-graders (abbr.)
34 Ferris wheel, e.g.
36 Harvard wall covering
37 Arced throw
38 Abbr. on the sports page
39 Faucet drip
40 "Big Daddy" Burl
42 Hindrance
44 Zorro's marks
45 Colorado ball-players
46 Comic canine barks
47 Haughty sorts

DOWN
1 Old commercial slogan (3 wds.)
2 Track meet feature
3 Rescue worker (abbr.)
4 Taxing time
5 Surveyed
6 Just due
7 Navigator's need
8 Patsy Cline hit (4 wds.)
9 Emergency
10 Mob
11 Politician Agnew
13 Look for bargains
19 Sale terms (2 wds.)
20 Santa smokes one
22 British trolley
24 Alphabetic quartet
27 Four-leaf __
28 Mistakes
29 Pigtail decorator
31 Racecourse shapes
32 Little kid
33 Henry Higgins's student
35 "Saturday Night Fever" music
39 Milk (Fr.)
41 Snaky sound
43 Ring verdict letters

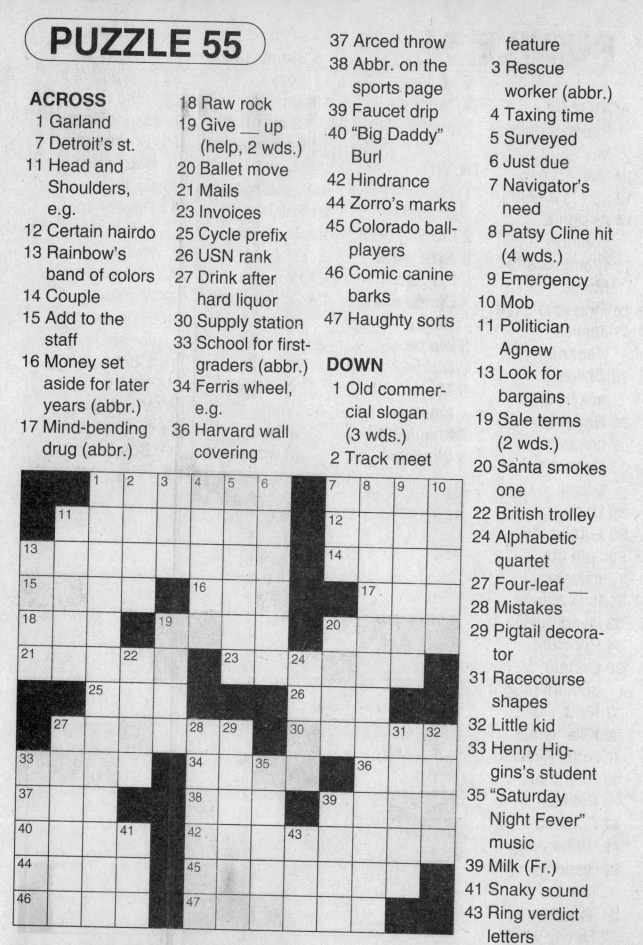

PUZZLE 56

ACROSS

1 Singer Mama __
5 Locales
10 Pleasant odor
12 January birth-stone
14 Sauntered
15 Inhabitant
16 Fifth sign of the zodiac
17 Shakespear-ean king
19 Envelope abbr.
20 Predict
22 Like King Cole
23 Whitewall, e.g.
24 Peaks
26 "Hurry up!"
28 Month units
29 "It's __ Way to Tipperary" (2 wds.)
30 Fountain drink
32 Speckle
33 Womanly
37 Tennis great Arthur
39 Doorway out
40 Work for AAA
41 Kitchen tool
43 Hosiery
45 Sikh's headgear
46 Detection device
47 Exams for high school juniors (abbr.)
48 Stocking shade

DOWN

1 Carved brooch
2 Bower
3 Scale note
4 Refining
5 "I want __..." (2 wds.)
6 Competed in the mile
7 Columnist Bombeck
8 "__ of a Murder"
9 Quiets
11 "Doe, __..." (2 wds.)
13 Takes care of
14 Politician Landon
18 Malt beverage
21 Famed English school
24 Simple arith-metic problem
25 James of "The Godfather"
26 Zoom-in shot
27 Some PTA members
29 Conform
30 "Masters of __"
31 Fails to include
33 Bouquet's background
34 "__ to Happen" (1936 George Raft film, 2 wds.)
35 __ Dame
36 Sounds of disgust
38 Idris of "The Wire"
42 Have supper
44 Large African antelope

PUZZLE 57

ACROSS

1 Modern office fixtures (abbr.)
4 Kettle by-product
9 Five __ chili
11 Sooner
14 Sticks and stones victims
15 Home of the Maple Leafs
16 Olden cry of surprise
17 Submissions to eds.
18 Part of Santa's laugh
19 Figure of speech
21 Printer's mark
22 Pampers (2 wds.)
25 Last-year students (abbr.)
26 Alternative to a Triscuit
28 Rule (abbr.)
31 Celebration
34 Mournful poem
36 Like vinegar
38 Throw
39 Cargo weight
41 2017 Pixar film
42 Worshiper
44 Undress
45 Forming droplets, as dew
46 Monopoly collections
47 Display lights
48 Many magazine pages

DOWN

1 "__ Hattie" (Porter musical)
2 Names at a movie's end
3 Some sweater sizes (abbr.)
4 Gels
5 Santa Fe Trail town
6 Stray
7 Luau farewell
8 Juveniles
9 Lincoln and Burrows
10 Sound reasoning
12 Anesthetic of the past
13 Plant parts
17 Actress Oberon
20 Tree adjective
21 Volcano-shaped
23 Main and Wall (abbr.)
24 Tycoon
27 Forced out
28 "This Old House" project, informally
29 Dodge
30 Bonn resident
32 Dresses up
33 Legal
35 Soar
37 Law officers
39 Memphis's state (abbr.)
40 Associations (abbr.)
43 "Blame It on __"
44 Mexican Mrs.

PUZZLE 58

ACROSS

1 Eyebrow shape
5 Bracelet catch
10 Current currencies, abroad
12 Schweitzer or Camus
14 The __ Family Singers
15 Garbage can "bandit"
17 Seize
18 Particles
20 Corporate money manager (abbr.)
21 Pacino and Capone
22 1916 Lopez hit
23 Heaviness
24 Military adjunct
25 Is defeated
26 Set in firmly
28 Past, for example
29 Miniature
30 Rug style
31 Bright and open
32 Water jug
33 Heartless man
36 Abbr. on a bank statement
37 Gussy up
38 "...bells on __ toes"
39 Rest and relaxation
41 Remove entirely
43 Team's good luck figure
44 Car heater setting
45 Rude glances
46 __ up (invigorates)

DOWN

1 Health care company
2 Opposite of urban
3 Ill-tempered persons
4 Pogo stick motion
5 Actress Lombard
6 Andean animal
7 Toddler's lesson
8 "Just a __!"
9 Procedure
11 Breed of dog
13 Chewy candy
16 Forget-me-__
19 Mary __ Lincoln
23 __ Kong
24 Well
25 Acquired knowledge
26 Marshall Mathers's more famous name
27 Word before arts or law
28 You, biblically
29 Boat canvas
30 Candy
32 Baseball boot
33 Rub against
34 Greek fable man
35 Sediment
37 Brownish-purple shade
40 Mariner's dir.
42 Pence, e.g. (abbr.)

PUZZLE 59

ACROSS

1 Injury
5 Grew older
9 Book of wares
12 Singer Perry
13 Unyielding
14 Speckled fish
16 Equips
17 Jungle fly
18 OT book (abbr.)
19 "Quiet!"
21 Bart Simpson's grades
22 Comic book protagonist, often
25 Letters on a dentist's sign
26 Staggering
28 ABC rival
31 Gas station sign (hyph.)
35 Hot tub sounds
37 Forget-me-___
38 Coach's group
39 Starts to flower, as a plant
41 Actress Taylor of "Mystic Pizza"
42 Playground attraction
43 Palm tree fruit
46 "Don't have ___!" (Bart Simpson quote, 2 wds.)
47 Groups of pupils
48 Mems. of Obama's party
49 Lincoln's coin

DOWN

1 Wheel-running rodent
2 ___ carte (2 wds.)
3 L. ___ Hubbard
4 The opposite of labor (abbr.)
5 Behaves
6 Having inset pieces, as a skirt
7 Showed feelings
8 Drenched
9 Pinochle necessities
10 Goodbye (Fr.)
11 Go back to base (2 wds.)
15 Dick Tracy's wife
17 Careful saving
19 Lusters
20 "Howdy!"
23 Dweller (abbr.)
24 Switch positions
27 "Scram!" (2 wds.)
28 Arrests
29 Sentimental song
30 Option
32 Bridle straps
33 Worth
34 Emanates
36 Wicked Biblical city
40 European gulls
43 300, to Cicero
44 Cry for the matador
45 Campbell's container

PUZZLE 60

ACROSS

1 Banned insecticide (abbr.)
4 __ cake
9 Bind (2 wds.)
11 Even chances
14 Live coal
15 "Blue Danube" country
16 Where to hear "Fresh Air" (abbr.)
17 Flaming
19 Compass letters
20 Heathcliff's portrayer
22 Strike, Biblically
24 Withstands
25 ...peas in __ (2 wds.)
26 Letter after bee
27 Label
29 Canadian province (abbr.)
32 Sentence stoppers
36 Burberry's pattern
38 Be humiliated (2 wds.)
39 "The Walking Dead" network
40 Knowledgeable
42 Doctors' gp.
43 Chewy confection
45 Actress Saoirse __
47 Offensive sight
48 Mystical people
49 Ate at eight
50 Coop inhabitant

DOWN

1 Cheek feature
2 Rubbish
3 Mon. follower
4 Flight of steps
5 Clock unit
6 Hairpin curves
7 Guess at a price (abbr.)
8 Item in a soup bunch
9 Choir singer
10 Extol
12 Tonto's horse, for example
13 Cut logs
18 Garden party
21 Lawrence of "Mama's Family"
23 David Copperfield's skill
27 Shred
28 Main channel
29 Astronaut's milieu
30 Skin care brand
31 Holy
32 Rang
33 Navel __
34 Land belonging to one person
35 Graceful birds
37 Matt of "True Grit"
41 Had been
44 "Do __ say!" (2 wds.)
46 Delighted cry

PUZZLE 61

ACROSS

1 Green orb
4 Maine's tree
8 Kilt's cousin
10 #1 hit for John Legend (3 wds.)
13 Suburban train
14 Nova Scotia's capital
15 Fleming and Hunter
16 Tyke
17 Not all
18 Manning or Wallach
19 Diggs of "Rent"
20 Blue flower
21 Tennis needs
23 Head (Fr.)
24 Motorists' gp.
25 Ballpark feats (abbr.)
26 Sedans, e.g.
28 Calmed
32 "The Saint" star Elisabeth
33 Native of Glasgow
34 Self
35 Yale's state (abbr.)
36 Slugger Williams
37 Prego's competition
38 Skilled craftsperson
40 Subway sandwiches
41 Like high schoolers
42 Isolated
43 Small rugs
44 Bounced check inits.

DOWN

1 Outing with food
2 Historical cycles
3 Large ocean
(abbr.)
4 Dish
5 "__ Cry Instead"
6 Least quiet
7 "E" for __
8 More sneaky
9 Australian animal
10 Sailors' greetings
11 First Lady before Jackie
12 Former spouses
16 British farewell (2 wds.)
19 Salada products
22 "Anna __"
23 Horse gait
25 "Robin __"
26 Allowance-earning task
27 She raised Dorothy Gale (2 wds.)
28 Panorama
29 Learn about (2 wds.)
30 Goad (2 wds.)
31 Immerse
32 "Go away!"
33 Male deer
37 Extended family (abbr.)
39 Sun. preceder
40 Harrison Ford role: __ Solo

PUZZLE 62

ACROSS

1 Oklahoma city
6 Singer Hayes
11 Caped Crusader
12 Actress Vivian
13 Olive stuffing
14 Madrid's location
15 Heidi's mountain
16 Boat blades
18 Hosp. figs.
19 552, to Ovid
21 Baby watchers
24 Tears apart
26 Football action
27 More tense
29 One of two in the throat
33 Bullring cries
35 Renowned march composer
36 Butcher shop items
39 Lose freshness
40 Quayle or Aykroyd
41 Pairs
43 Rat-a-__
44 "That's __ how-do-you-do!" (2 wds.)
47 Sea mollusk
49 Readapt
50 Esteem
51 Backstreet Boys' rivals
52 Animal snares

DOWN

1 Packing down firmly
2 Beehive State tribe
3 K followers
4 Underworld figure
5 Parka
6 ICU hookups (abbr.)
7 Gullible person
8 "What's in __?" (2 wds.)
9 Etching fluids
10 100-year periods (abbr.)
11 Sent an invoice
13 Father, Spanish-style
17 Peevish mood
20 Senseless sort
22 Service stripers (abbr.)
23 "That's no surprise" (2 wds.)
25 Offer for money
28 Actor Robert
30 They come a-calling
31 Oahu, e.g.
32 Starbucks order
34 "__ Little" (E.B. White book)
36 Coffee houses
37 Make whole
38 Staid
40 Mend argyles
42 Long story
45 Diarist Anaïs
46 List shortener (abbr.)
48 Fold (over)

PUZZLE 63

ACROSS

1 Trial software
5 Beautiful Disney heroine
10 Explosions (hyph.)
13 Be of value to
14 Went back on a promise
15 Striped Christmas candies
16 Devours
17 Hasty
19 Hwy. crime
20 Forelimb
21 Personal welfare
22 Dust particle
23 Prepared to propose
25 Treble ___
27 Pig's nose
29 Labors hard
31 Fork feature
32 Sorrow
34 Diagnosis tools (abbr.)
36 Bird coop
39 TX to NY dir.
40 Hugs on a card
41 Blender noise
42 College sports gp.
43 Dressing variety
45 Restarts the computer
47 Disparaging
48 Young, aspiring actress
49 ___ Lauder of cosmetics
50 "___ for All Seasons" (2 wds.)

DOWN

1 "My pleasure!" (3 wds.)
2 Meadow mamas
3 Cocoa holder
4 "Aida," for one
5 Johann Sebastian ___
6 ___ Marie Saint
7 Nickname for Illinois (3 wds.)
8 U.S. Navy officer (abbr.)
9 Borden animal
10 Shatter
11 Acquires knowledge
12 Neighbor of Wyo.
18 Denomination
21 Shock
22 Israeli stateswoman Golda
24 "Hi and ___"
26 Theater box
28 High-___
30 Lawmaking group
33 Big meal
34 Telegraphers' ___ code
35 Certain horses
37 Snobbish ways
38 Actress Garbo
41 Roller coaster exclamation
42 Ephron or Charles
44 Alphabetic trio
46 Emeril's exclamation

PUZZLE 64

ACROSS

1 "__ the nerve!" (2 wds.)
6 Recipe direction (2 wds.)
11 Tyler Perry character
12 Actor Barrymore
14 Had the flu
15 Writing instruments
17 Heredity letters
18 Actor Damon
19 Inventor's monogram
20 Tiny mints (2 wds.)
23 Wistful phrase (2 wds.)
24 Mystical exercise
25 Ovine complaint
26 Bestows
29 "Be it __ humble..." (2 wds.)
30 Jeans brand
31 Nav. VIP
32 Cartel letters
33 Train signal
36 __ Marino
37 Decoy
38 Actor McKellen
40 First name of Freud

42 Game played in a church hall
44 Official ruling
45 Play the __
46 Orange peelings
47 Forest rangers' problems

DOWN

1 Actor Epps of "House"
2 Dim, as light
3 Dwight's opponent
4 Golf great Trevino
5 Chap
6 Silky wool
7 Eats sparingly
8 "__ Stop"
9 Business collaborative (abbr.)
10 Nor's partner
13 Andes animals
16 Take care of (2 wds.)
18 "Life," "Time," "OK!," etc. (abbr.)
21 Skeptical one
22 Tater __
23 Warn

25 Some men's undies
26 Lip application
27 Settled a loan
28 Retribution seeker
29 Give off
31 Reprimands
33 Dwindled
34 Ocean vessel
35 Bird on quarters
37 Scorch
39 Drowses
41 1,101, to Caesar
42 Bosom buddy, to a texter
43 Sundial's 3

PUZZLE 65

ACROSS

1 Chew
5 Lighting devices
10 Start for active or rocket
12 Breakfast dish
14 Hurt
15 On the ball
16 1004, in old Rome
17 Quartet following B
19 CPR experts
20 Wimbledon wear
22 Cherished animal
23 One of four on a car
24 Crossword hints
26 "Hurry up!"
28 Klutz's cry
29 Loud, ringing sound
30 Gangster's girl
32 That man's
33 One with a large appetite (2 wds.)
37 Part of CPA (abbr.)
39 Paddles
40 Justice Fortas
41 Cloaks' kin
43 Ran off to wed
45 Deserves
46 More secure
47 Annie's pup
48 Skin growth

DOWN

1 Wheat, for one
2 Pluck
3 Modern cash dispenser (abbr.)
4 Destroying
5 Idles
6 Early hrs.
7 Parcel (out)
8 Fatten (2 wds.)
9 Parlor pieces
11 Stranger
13 Tryouts
14 "__ Pinafore"
18 Prior, to poets
21 Like __ of bricks (2 wds.)
24 Popular side dish
25 "Damn Yankees" temptress
26 Stereotyped phrases
27 Maybelline cosmetic
29 Narrow gorge
30 Farrow of films
31 Fairy tale monsters
33 Pushy
34 Thin candle
35 Reviewer Roger
36 Stop sign color
38 Mattress size
42 British partnership abbr.
44 The chance __ lifetime (2 wds.)

PUZZLE 66

ACROSS

1 Rights group (abbr.)
6 Quartet after E
10 Tokyo entertainer
11 Golden-voiced Vaughan
12 Facing charges (2 wds.)
13 Resort south of Salt Lake City
14 Line
15 "The Lion King" lion
17 Brisk energy
18 College VIP
20 Garish light
21 O'Toole, e.g. (abbr.)
22 Do military stints
24 Barrett of gossip
26 Potato peeler's discards
28 Comic Milton
31 Taking it easy
33 Uprisings
35 Play division
38 Long, wriggly fish
40 Braff of "Garden State"
41 Sheep's noise
42 Skilled
44 Still, to a poet
45 Register
47 Subdued completely
49 Amy or Abigail
50 Oil transporter
51 Cast
52 Sticks around

DOWN

1 CBS or NBC
2 Televise
3 Possibly flawed (2 wds.)
4 Daisy __
5 Golfer Arnold __
6 "The __ Side"
7 Feel one's way
8 New __, Connecticut
9 Spots for eating flapjacks
10 Earth-dwelling goblins
11 Wrench
12 Globes
16 Dunce
19 107, to Caesar
23 Makes beloved
25 Goldwater's home st.
27 Arctic vehicle
29 Detests
30 Engraver
32 Votes in
34 Ready for cantering
35 "My Heart Skips __" (2 wds.)
36 "No prob!" (2 wds.)
37 British farewells (2 wds.)
39 Lean eater Jack
43 StarKist product
46 Mommy's three
48 Blue yonder

PUZZLE 67

ACROSS

1 Taunt
5 Blubbers
10 Novelist Jong
11 Shouts of joy
13 ___ in (covers snugly)
14 One of the Marx Brothers
16 Like tired muscles
17 Weaving appliance
18 Charged particle
19 Flower wreath
20 Duluth's locale (abbr.)
21 Barn's setting
22 Topic
24 Bowling lane
25 "Jezebel" singer Frankie
26 Pass over
27 Fists, slangily
28 Montezuma, e.g.
29 "By Jove!"
30 Cry of regret
31 Passports, e.g. (abbr.)
34 Abby's sister
35 Blender noise
36 Believe
37 Cleaning cloth
39 Three-card ___
40 Bar
41 Roast host
42 Smooths wood
43 Unpleasant look

DOWN

1 Armistice
2 Air Capital of the World (2 wds.)
3 Gross
4 Professors' helpers (abbr.)
5 Past
6 Baseball's Hank
7 Personal pronoun
8 ___ Gehrig
9 Anthropology, for one (2 wds.)
10 Kin of etc. (2 wds.)
12 Strands
15 "___ Own" (2 wds.)
17 Key ___ pie
20 Clothing store section
21 Floating frozen mass
23 Hastened
24 ___ and crafts
25 It holds a wheel in place (2 wds.)
26 Former Russian leader
27 Mideast sea
28 Straightens
30 "___ Day's Night" (2 wds.)
32 Prevent
33 Captain Hook's lackey
35 Plain bird
36 Stadium covering
38 Dam-building agcy.
39 Director ___ Brooks

PUZZLE 68

ACROSS

1 Rock's Turner
5 Wound mementos
10 Maxim
13 Tanker
14 Newborn's outfit
15 Finger, e.g.
16 States of excitement
17 Fleming and Richardson
19 Out __ limb (2 wds.)
20 D.C. MLB player
21 Head (Fr.)
22 Purple flower
23 One of a car's pedals
25 Abate
27 Appended (2 wds.)
29 Actor Martin __
31 Horse compartment
35 Give over
36 Poi source
38 A-U linkup
39 Thurman of "Kill Bill"
40 Curse
41 Tramped
42 Slightly drunk
44 Putting forth
46 Release
47 Place for

military planes (2 wds.)
48 Gnats, e.g.
49 Christmas carol

DOWN

1 Celica maker
2 Currier & __
3 Meshed snare
4 Clarinetist Shaw
5 Puts down pregrown grass
6 102, to Nero
7 Clinton's vice president (2 wds.)
8 Restrain (2 wds.)
9 Girls of Spain (abbr.)
10 Alternative course of action (2 wds.)
11 Detection device
12 Extreme passion for the Fab Four
18 "People who __ people..."
21 Koppel and Kennedy
22 "__ She Lovely"
24 Cabbage-like plant
26 Fair (hyph.)
28 Computer input
29 Valentine inscription (2 wds.)
30 Modifies
32 Rooftop sight
33 Roaring critters
34 Mountain cabin
35 Joker
37 Varnish-making substance
40 Farewells
41 Hollow cylinder
43 Make a lap
45 Sign in the theater district (abbr.)

PUZZLE 69

ACROSS

1 Florida city
6 __ throat
11 __ lettuce
13 Onionlike plant
14 Like a Bedouin
15 Adjust back to zero
16 Horned viper
17 Actress Irving
18 Portents
19 Iron alloy
21 Spark-producing rock
22 Deserves
23 Bandleader Lawrence
24 Rugged cliff
25 Author Talese
26 In the matter of (2 wds.)
30 Certain PCs
32 Talk off-the-cuff (hyph.)
33 Seaside sights
35 Dispositions
36 Lease again
37 Highest card
39 Treat for Jack Horner
40 Group of eight musicians
41 High school pep boosters
43 Slugger Bonds
44 Quakers
45 Couturier Bill
46 Inelegant language

DOWN

1 Type of paint
2 Lawyers' gp.
3 Olympians' awards
4 Stiffly formal
5 Word in CIA (abbr.)
6 Rolled-up document
7 Gilbert and Sullivan work (2 wds.)
8 Ascended
9 Social occasion
10 Vet's clients
11 "Coming!" (3 wds.)
12 Ginger, to Fred
20 Locomotive drivers
21 Tina of "30 Rock"
23 "Kilroy __ here"
25 Weight units (abbr.)
27 Slanting
28 Neatened
29 Become fixated
31 Boop et al.
32 Earhart of the air
33 Transferable picture
34 Extreme (prefix)
36 Lynda Bird's married name
37 Sounds of barking
38 Sagan or Sandburg
42 Cariou of "Blue Bloods"

PUZZLE 70

ACROSS

1 Emulated
5 Great bargain
10 Type of bow tie (hyph.)
12 Hooded snakes
14 What one's wearing
15 If all goes right (2 wds.)
16 Period between wars
18 Skinny ___ rail (2 wds.)
19 Sets for "The Good Doctor" and "ER" (abbr.)
20 Peak (abbr.)
21 ___ badge
23 Legal claim
24 Regrets
25 "___-hoo!" (attention-getting call)
27 Lower the lights
29 Some sizes (abbr.)
30 "Downton Abbey" countess
31 Negative reply
33 Destroys
35 Dog's warning
36 Musician's deg.
39 La Plata's locale (abbr.)
40 Punishing spoonful (2 wds.)
43 Halted
45 Overrun
46 Robe for Madame Butterfly
47 "Parted" water (2 wds.)
48 Colors lightly
49 Monopoly holding

DOWN

1 Take in or let out
2 Mideast breads
3 Grand
4 "Sound of Music" song (hyph.)
5 Shell game, e.g.
6 ___ pole
7 Taper off
8 Alternative to carpeting (2 wds.)
9 Scottish girls
10 Mob VIP
11 Cleared a profit
13 ERA, HR, and RBI, e.g.
17 Baseball periods
22 A Gardner
23 Money expected back
25 Tag player's call (2 wds.)
26 Paper-folding craft
28 Bricklayer's mixture
30 Break
32 Examined
34 Bloodhound's clue
36 Small rodent
37 Imposed penalties
38 "M*A*S*H" actor
41 Hubbubs
42 Came by horse
44 Daughter's counterpart

PUZZLE 71

ACROSS
1 Gp. for seniors
5 Grand hotel lobby
11 Halloween spirit
13 Disinfect
14 Marisa of "My Cousin Vinny"
15 Modified, as laws
16 HBO alternative
17 Tight
18 File folder features
20 Rings out
24 Legendary gunfight site (2 wds.)
28 552, to Ovid
29 ___ Jima
30 Singer Shore
32 Online exclamation
33 Cinema's Turner
35 Home of the NHL's Oilers
37 Colander
39 Artist Salvador
40 "Leave ___ Beaver" (2 wds.)
42 Major airline
46 Traffic menace (2 wds.)
49 Cooler
50 Auction house employees
51 Ridicule
52 Sweater pattern
53 Sp. unmarried woman

DOWN
1 Representatives (abbr.)
2 "There'll be ___ time..." (2 wds.)
3 Actress Downey
4 ___ Vallarta
5 ___ mater
6 Prepare to play golf (2 wds.)
7 Talked wildly
8 Neighbor of Ky.
9 Exploit
10 TV's "Chicago ___"
12 Long-tailed reptile
13 Raining ___ (teeming, 3 wds.)
19 Camembert look-alike
21 "Thanks ___!" (2 wds.)
22 Luxury car rental
23 Posted direction
24 Fixes a squeak
25 River in a movie title
26 Geometric shape
27 Buddhist monk
31 "Stop right there!" (2 wds.)
34 With enthusiasm
36 Brother's daughters
38 Singer Merman
41 Shredded
43 Prevaricator
44 School final
45 Vicinity
46 Magnavox rival
47 Dinghy accessory
48 Math branch (abbr.)

PUZZLE 72

ACROSS

1 "__ to Happen" (1936 George Raft film, 2 wds.)
6 "__ Excited" (Pointer Sisters, 2 wds.)
10 Not those
11 San Francisco team
14 Counters in many drug-stores, once (2 wds.)
17 Chile's neighbor (abbr.)
18 Actress West et al.
19 Thompson of "Caroline in the City"
20 Tidies up
23 Fishing spot
24 Foolishly excited
25 Tony of "Taxi"
26 Brand of corn oil
29 "Murphy Brown" star Candice
30 Dry as __ (2 wds.)
31 Barn dwellers
32 Former NYC mayor __ Giuliani
33 Snappy come-backs
36 TV show with NY and Miami spin-offs
37 Add to the staff
38 Modern music category
40 Hopelessly in love (3 wds.)
44 Famous evolution trial
45 Creme-filled cookies
46 Figure skater Katarina
47 Didn't exist

DOWN

1 "__ living" (2 wds.)
2 Prickle
3 Shrub barrier
4 Cool __ cucumber (2 wds.)
5 C followers
6 Large lizard
7 Coal pits
8 Pre-college exams (abbr.)
9 __ wing and a prayer (2 wds.)
12 Laying a bathroom floor
13 Cold symptom
15 Alpha's counterpart
16 Clinging wrap
21 Suffering
22 Legend
23 Kitchen gadget
25 Art __
26 Windy month
27 Takes advantage of, in a way
28 "Horoscope Guide" chart
29 Nibbler
31 Least
33 Fasten firmly
34 Forest growths
35 Stylist's "office"
37 Arizona tribe
39 Attention-getting sound
41 __ Jones average
42 __-to
43 Historical time frame

ACROSS
1 Prior, in verse
4 Comrade
8 Disapproving sounds
12 Calendar abbr.
13 Astronauts' gp.
14 Words of dismay (2 wds.)
15 Resident of Nantucket
17 Brit's buggy
18 Fuel source
19 __ the Red
21 Heroic pilot
22 Cherokee, Sioux, etc.
24 Move furtively
26 Low card
27 Pepe le Pew et al.
28 Prepares leftovers
30 Wave or toss, e.g.
32 Terse
35 Dwayne Johnson Disney movie
36 Place to dab perfume
38 Cottonseed __
39 Battleship color
41 "Jane __" (Brontë book)
42 Keyed up
44 Maid's necessities (2 wds.)
46 Whetstone
47 British school
48 Allow
49 "Back in the __" (Beatles)
50 "__ It Make My Brown Eyes Blue"
51 Filthy area

DOWN
1 Public proclamation
2 Vacation hotel
3 Bakery treat
4 Wolf Blitzer's network
5 Greek god of the underworld
6 Employer
7 Hargitay of "SVU"
8 Summit
9 Got smaller in the dryer
10 Special aptitudes
11 A handful
16 Canadian province
20 Type of purse
23 Looking at
25 Underwriter
27 Member of Congress (abbr.)
29 Salted away
30 Buddies, in Chihuahua
31 Punctuation marks
33 Kansas City baseballers
34 Butt
36 Actress Cicely
37 Touchy
38 Home of the Aloha Bowl
40 Ford product
43 Where Berlin is (abbr.)
45 Blaster's need (abbr.)

PUZZLE 74

ACROSS

1 Issue a challenge
5 Over yonder
9 "This __ stickup!" (2 wds.)
12 __ tea
13 "Penny __"
14 Bert Bobbsey's twin
15 Hoagies' kin
16 Go to bat for (2 wds.)
18 Brook
20 Certain auto tires
21 Assert
23 Ruse
24 Kitty noise
26 Word in RPM
27 Sked fillers
30 At __ (puzzled, 2 wds.)
32 Friar's title
33 Caesar's attire
35 Throw __ (flip out, 2 wds.)
36 Tankard material
40 Wrong answer
43 Mentioned
45 Preparing a T-bone, perhaps
47 Soda option
48 Letters between K and O
49 Oz creator L. Frank __
50 Elevator pioneer
51 Road curve
52 Egyptian snakes
53 Actor Green

DOWN

1 The "D" in CD
2 Lexus rival
3 Resist authority
4 Old Ford
5 Heidi's peak
6 Prettier
7 Kendrick or Paquin
8 Got, for short
9 Breathes in
10 Bluejackets
11 Raring to go
17 Large African animal, informally
19 Held on to
22 Blast of wind
25 Intense anger
27 States positively
28 Sing Sing et al.
29 Songbird Page
31 Mower's target
34 Unlock (2 wds.)
35 Walk leisurely
37 Tex-Mex snacks
38 Be theatrical
39 Rekindled
41 Actress Jessica
42 Korean cars
44 Morse Code component
46 MLB execs

PUZZLE 75

ACROSS

1 Notify
7 Computer keyboard key
11 Pupil covering
12 Prying bars
15 Light bulb inventor
16 Foot part
17 9-digit item (abbr.)
18 Writer Leon ("Exodus")
20 Govt. agcy.
21 Sheet music sign (2 wds.)
24 "___ over my head" (2 wds.)
25 Messenger
26 Pitt and others
27 Toe the line
28 Ox collar
29 Escapes
30 Made amends
32 Wrest
33 North African country west of Egypt
34 Wind dir.
35 Anti-fur org.
37 Dentist's degree (abbr.)
40 GI's ___ bag
42 Casanovas
45 Oil tanker mishaps
46 Café ___ (2 wds.)
47 London gallery
48 Clown props

DOWN

1 Sherbets
2 Grows sleepy
3 Perk (2 wds.)
4 Light switch positions
5 Olden car
6 Panama's Noriega
7 152, to Caesar
8 Addition "place"
9 Campers' vehicles (abbr.)
10 Monty Hall show (4 wds.)
13 Dwelled
14 Reaches across
19 "Mayberry, ___"
22 Code of beliefs
23 Puts down tile
24 Light sarcasm
25 Hides, slangily (2 wds.)
26 Party request (abbr.)
29 Gwynne and Willard
30 Flight height (abbr.)
31 Beauty pageant crowns
35 Fur trader's item
36 "Or ___!"
38 ___-yourself (hyph.)
39 Grounded jets (abbr.)
41 Disney World's locale (abbr.)
43 "Begone!"
44 1,051 in old Rome

PUZZLE 76

ACROSS

1 Treatises
7 Part of NATO (abbr.)
10 Chewy candies
12 Apportioned
15 Food unit
16 Throw about
17 Choose
18 Tug
20 Jai __
21 Paper measures
23 Beaming
25 __ St. Vincent Millay
26 Sevareid and Ambler
27 British beverage
30 Gp. once headed by Heston
31 Apology word
33 Detergent brand
37 Baseball arbiters
39 Fang injection
40 Give the impression
41 Rani's wear
43 Addition answer
44 Palatial resi-dence
46 Very talkative
48 NBA game spot
49 Shoulder decoration
50 Coloring fluid
51 Born first

DOWN

1 Repeat
2 Lathered
3 Former Turkish ruler
4 Past
5 Lawns
6 Cookbook verb
7 Causes of bounced checks (abbr.)
8 Avenge
9 __ bread
11 Ionian and Ross
13 Tilts
14 Nest-building bit
19 Feds (hyph.)
22 Wedlock
24 Bargain bin abbr.
28 Do the wrong thing
29 Supportive
31 Blur
32 Unsealed
34 Sneaker part
35 Drenches
36 Clown Kelly
37 Cadets' college (abbr.)
38 Hold on to
39 Like a social media phe-nomenon
42 Seized vehicle, for short
45 Norma or Charlotte
47 Little bloomer

ACROSS

1 Nordic capital
5 Charts
9 Talia's "Rocky" role
11 "Cheers" waitress
13 Apartment alternative (2 wds.)
16 One against
17 Milk sources
18 Authors' submissions (abbr.)
19 As well
20 Lucy's '50s costar
21 Guideline, for short
22 Went astray
24 Author Hemingway
26 Linger
28 Very long period
29 Dr. who turned into Mr. Hyde
32 Take in an orphan
36 Gallops
37 Every's partner
39 Double this for a dance
40 Banned insec-
ticide (abbr.)
41 "State __"
42 Restraining influence
43 With an insulting tone
46 Timex alternative
47 Brunch beverage
48 Smooth
49 Fence feature

DOWN

1 One who speaks in public
2 Apple "helper"
3 Young fellow
4 In storage
(2 wds.)
5 Baseball slugger Mark
6 Tongue-depressor sounds
7 Golf course employee
8 Batters sometimes have them
9 Ease up
10 Generous sort
12 Plus
14 Clown's red squeaker
15 PC key
20 6/6/44 (hyph.)
21 Telegraph
23 Caribous' cousins
25 Biblical patriarch
27 The Great One of TV
29 First name in betrayal
30 Pre-dessert dish
31 Milk (Fr.)
33 Swift cat
34 Collins and Donahue
35 Actress Roberts
36 Streets (abbr.)
38 Pinch piecrust
41 Fraud
42 Collides
44 104, to Caesar
45 AFL's partner

PUZZLE 78

ACROSS

1 Papas' mates
6 Zeus's warrior daughter
12 Cuban capital
13 Called on a rotary phone
14 Pizza topping
15 Fearful
16 Soccer great Hamm
17 Electrical unit in physics
19 Sates
20 James of jazz
22 Lawyers' gp.
24 Capacity
25 George ___ Shaw
29 Super Bowl III MVP (2 wds.)
31 Self-___ (confident)
32 Trial figure (abbr.)
34 Certain sweater sizes (abbr.)
35 Very uncommon
36 Red as ___ (2 wds.)
40 "PAW Patrol" fan
43 Professors' helpers (abbr.)
44 Serving spoons
46 Law enforce-

ment officers
48 Pincers
49 Brokers
50 Strainers
51 Yearns

DOWN

1 Winnipeg's province
2 Pilots
3 Chinese leader
4 The A of A.D.
5 Dress's belt
6 Dentists' gp.
7 Name on a famous jewelry store
8 Spy Mata ___
9 Airline to the Mideast (2 wds.)
10 Playwright Simon
11 Increases
12 Painter Winslow
18 "I'm No Angel" star (2 wds.)
21 "Famous" cookie maker
23 Country singer Paisley
25 Sleeping qtrs.
26 Not quite shut
27 Revolving
28 Takes away
(from)
30 Harsh
33 Positive answers
36 Lake Geneva peaks
37 Indonesian island
38 Falco or McClurg
39 Abbr. on a mountain sign
41 Luminous stone
42 Take-out phrase (2 wds.)
45 Draft agcy.
47 Actor Cariou

PUZZLE 79

ACROSS

1 Musical staff symbols
6 __ d'Azur
10 Hulk __
11 Excite
13 Admire greatly
14 Every 12 months
15 Online exclamation
16 Canadian symbol (2 wds.)
18 Slugger's hope (abbr.)
19 Winter sportsman
20 Former fast jet (abbr.)
21 Lincoln's coin
23 Overly proper person
25 One who debates
28 Assuage
32 Alimony payers
34 Work
35 College deg.
38 Sorbonne setting
41 "__ live and breathe!" (2 wds.)
42 Spanish city
44 Holy men (abbr.)
45 Take away by force
46 Samuel of the Supreme Court
48 Like some winter weather
49 __ a dull moment
50 Completes
51 Buffing board material

DOWN

1 Bedroom
2 Shelter
3 Freud's concern
4 Works the soil
5 Approach stealthily
6 British "bye-bye"
7 Vocalized
8 Akron output
9 Fitzgerald et al.
11 President John and author Anne
12 Alternative to Uber
15 Black-and-white whale
17 Card spot
22 Mon. follower
24 "He __ Game"
26 Anticipates
27 Property
29 Appliance for browning bread
30 Study of the past
31 Actor Wallach et al.
33 Sign in the theater district (abbr.)
35 Advanced degs.
36 Aesop story
37 Cosmetic brand: Elizabeth __
39 Foolish
40 Witch trial town
43 Gave a hint
47 Possessive contraction

PUZZLE 80

ACROSS

1 __-league baseball
6 Finish second
11 Headache relief brand
12 Certificate of graduation
14 Ort
15 Systematic plan
16 Hoops great __ Malone
17 "__ the Explorer"
18 "A-Team" member (2 wds.)
19 Snoop
20 Golf instructors
21 Gear teeth
22 Gateway
24 Without company
25 Outer wrap
26 Refried beans ingredient
27 Little tykes
28 Youngster
30 Prez's military role (abbr.)
31 Large serpents
32 Soccer mom's transport
34 Coffee vessel
35 It spreads disease
36 Evening, in adspeak
37 Indignant outcry (2 wds.)
39 Group of temporary deputies
40 Cornmeal side dish
41 Orally
42 Tiny pests
43 Complains

DOWN

1 Covers up
2 Abner Yokum's creator (2 wds.)
3 "Crossing Jordan" actor (2 wds.)
4 Face shape
5 GOP party (abbr.)
6 Wharves' kin
7 Links gp.
8 Muhammad __
9 3, to 21 and 33, for example (2 wds.)
10 Come out into view
12 Dribble
13 Picnic crashers
17 "Phooey!"
20 School gps.
21 Parachute part
23 Univ. military group
24 Fellows
26 Neeson of films
27 Lose interest in (2 wds.)
28 Seoul's locale
29 Devours (2 wds.)
30 Turning point
31 Lahr et al.
33 Necessities
35 Actress Rowlands
36 Lopez's theme song
38 Laughter syllable
39 Hawaii's ocean (abbr.)

PUZZLE 81

ACROSS

1 Treaties
6 Press down
10 Adores
13 Draft status (hyph.)
14 Roof
15 "Me, myself, __" (2 wds.)
16 Peculiar
17 Miami resident, e.g.
19 Bullring "rah"
20 Makes do
21 City rails
22 Ink holders
24 Stainers
26 "That's all there __ it!" (2 wds.)
27 Type of type (abbr.)
31 Lively dance
36 Mama's counterpart
37 Turf
40 Will not
41 DVD player button
42 January markdown event (2 wds.)
45 Disapproving sound
46 Othello's enemy
47 Assess
49 Forbidding
50 Abdicated
51 Level-headed
52 Bachelor parties

DOWN

1 Sensible
2 Mule's cousin
3 Professional cook
4 Named, as a book
5 Haunted house description
6 Kermit's cousin
7 Sharpshooter Oakley
8 Olympian's award
9 Back woes
10 Actress Goldberg
11 Scads
12 Shopping tour
18 Jerusalem's country (abbr.)
23 Drench
25 Funnyman Caesar
28 Scottish plaids
29 "__ Fideles"
30 Needed
32 Fall into debt
33 Also-ran
34 Rascals
35 Finally (2 wds.)
37 Gulps
38 Scarlett's surname
39 "Let's eat!" (2 wds.)
43 "You Belong __" (2 wds.)
44 "On the Waterfront" director Kazan
48 Soft boot brand

PUZZLE 82

ACROSS

1 Mimics
6 Luke's dad on "Modern Family"
10 Photography equipment
11 Bea Arthur TV role
12 Belching
13 Jimmy of the "Daily Planet"
14 Letters before U
15 Strictness
17 Topeka's st.
18 "Oh, what fun __ to ride..." (2 wds.)
20 Rodent-sighting sounds
21 Cagey
22 Christmas check
24 TV's Carey
26 Famed rapper
28 Juneau's state
32 Picket-line crosser
34 Garden pest
35 Circle part
38 Annoy
40 Use a keyboard
41 Call on
42 Correct copy
44 Flowery season (abbr.)
45 Interweave
47 Till now (3 wds.)
49 Playbill lists
50 Cookie __
51 Cutting tools
52 Listens to

DOWN

1 007's drink
2 Tiny terror
3 Israeli stateswoman Golda
4 Tennessee __ Ford
5 Drooped
6 Comrade
7 Corn shucker's discards
8 Utopian
9 Bruce or Kravitz
10 Habit
11 Tasty tidbits
12 Payola payment
16 Green pods for gumbo
19 Phoenix sports team
23 Undisclosed matters
25 Long for
27 Disfigure
29 Agrees to (2 wds.)
30 Cured herring
31 Attentive
33 Laundry whitener
35 Animal rights gp.
36 Let go of tension
37 Stop
39 Come afterward
43 Be lavish with love
46 "__ a Wonderful Life"
48 Flower-sending letters

PUZZLE 83

ACROSS

1 Recipe abbr.
5 They can be plastic or paper
9 Moronic
12 Immigration island
14 Mixed-breed dog
15 Loud
16 Soda __
17 It's north of Mex.
18 Pennies
19 Make into law
21 Rooter's shout
23 The Tigers, on score-boards (abbr.)
24 Former NBC nighttime host
25 Train rider's snack spot (2 wds.)
27 Arafat's gp.
29 Happy __ lark (2 wds.)
30 State troop-er's quarry
33 Keystone __
37 It follows fa
38 Make stitches
39 Repeating series
40 Readies, briefly
42 Artist and singer Yoko
44 Greek letter
45 "Thereby hangs __" (2 wds.)
46 Seoul natives
48 Tree gum
49 Doesn't feed
50 Bart Simp-son's grades
51 In other cir-cumstances

DOWN

1 __ Alley (2 wds.)
2 Swamp's kin
3 Swaggering walk
4 Slapstick missiles
5 Seats in the park
6 Burn-soothing plant
7 Billie's "Oz" role
8 Mary-Kate, to Ashley
9 Drive forward
10 "Lorna __"
11 "Nutcracker" girl
13 Method (abbr.)
20 Manage
22 At a distance
25 "The Da Vinci __"
26 Opposite of moist, in brownies
28 Diminishes
30 Arranged
31 Child's "magic word"
32 "Return of the Jedi" creatures
34 In music, from do to do
35 Flat surface
36 Dr. __ (chil-dren's writer)
37 Sail support
39 Deep orange-pink hue
41 Ballet exercise
43 Written reminder
47 Sounds of hesitation

PUZZLE 84

ACROSS

1 Large musical instrument
5 Ruses
10 Frog's resting spot (2 wds.)
13 Actress Perez
14 May birthstone
15 Pepper or ginger, e.g.
16 Lhasa __
17 Crybaby's sound
19 Cloth measure
20 Kilmer of "Tombstone"
21 Fox's HQ
22 Baseball's Slaughter
23 Kane on "All My Children"
25 Some California cops (abbr.)
27 Sirloins, e.g.
29 Sounds
33 Philosopher Descartes
35 Imprint
36 __ California (Mexican peninsula)
39 Humble reply to a compliment (2 wds.)
41 Opponent
42 Grad, informally
43 "We __ People..."
44 London art gallery
45 Longtime Chicago mayor
47 Neglected
49 Talk __ a minute (2 wds.)
50 Unposed snapshots
51 "To us!," e.g.
52 Husky transport

DOWN

1 Novice
2 __ creek (2 wds.)
3 Light wood
4 Lubricate (2 wds.)
5 Certain upperclassmen (abbr.)
6 Look for errors
7 From Vietnam or China
8 Small (prefix)
9 Plant beginnings
10 Fall fallers
11 Divulge
12 Jones of "Saturday Night Live"
18 __ muffin
21 Salt __ City
24 Very chewy candies
26 Bouquet unit
28 Sour mood
30 African expedition
31 Gushed
32 Accelerates
34 Moral principles
36 Lacking a knack for (2 wds.)
37 Texas shrine
38 Child or Roberts
40 Stately
44 "Sweeney __"
46 Thus far
48 Compass point (abbr.)

PUZZLE 85

ACROSS

1 Lupino and Tarbell
5 Flats' counterparts
11 A one
14 Conical tents
15 "Be it __ humble..." (2 wds.)
16 TV host Dahl
17 Olympic awards
18 Thing, in grammar
19 "__ creature was stirring..." (2 wds.)
21 British __
24 Close tie
27 Gomer Pyle's org.
29 Give __ go (2 wds.)
30 Pub drink
31 Zodiac sign
32 Hog's abode
33 Cloth scrap
34 Lipstick shades
35 School orgs.
36 MetLife competitor
38 Jacob's twin brother
40 "As far as __ tell..." (2 wds.)
42 Strolled
46 Eastern temple
48 Abundant
49 Breakfast dish
50 Puzzle
51 __ fly
52 Certain fuel

DOWN

1 Piece
2 Plunge
3 Imitated
4 Run aground
5 Jazz saxophonist Getz
6 Vainglorious behavior
7 Outstanding mark (2 wds.)
8 Sign on again
9 Ink holder
10 Mariner's dir.
12 Norway's capital
13 Stance
20 All kidding __
22 Comics' Kett
23 Vocalizes
24 Vamp Theda
25 Lovable "Frozen" character
26 Lady's robe
28 Telegram, e.g.
31 Pinball palaces
35 Not private
37 Frisky as __ (2 wds.)
39 "__ Called Horse" (2 wds.)
41 Nickname for Nathan
43 Company's emblem
44 Columnist Bombeck
45 Transaction
46 __ roast
47 Morning hours (abbr.)

PUZZLE 86

ACROSS

1 Food, informally
5 Makes a selection
9 Des __
11 Journey
12 British soldier, informally
13 Present time
15 He played Pierce on "M*A*S*H"
16 Ingredient of guacamole
18 "Annabel Lee" poet
19 Skye, e.g.
21 Type of school (abbr.)
22 Urgency
25 __ World (amusement park)
26 Avoids
30 Camaraderie
32 Showed up
35 British title
36 Gin inventor Whitney
37 Most needy
39 Manitoba Nation
40 Musician Shaw
41 Pinched
44 __ kit
45 Stays at home for supper (2 wds.)
46 Airport abbrs.
47 Look over

DOWN

1 Athena or Hera
2 Costa __
3 __, dos, tres...
4 "Maude" star Arthur
5 Filmdom's Preminger
6 Total amount brought in
7 Wave type
8 Playing card marking
9 Christopher of "Law & Order: SVU"
10 Rancid
12 Speedy
14 __ Kippur
17 Seller
19 Psychic's phrase (2 wds.)
20 Passing fashions
23 Of lesser quality
24 Hood
27 Vlasic product
28 Actress Brennan
29 Emulated Bond
31 Foamy coffee
32 Tax figurer (abbr.)
33 Blood channel
34 Outboard __
38 "Electric" swimmers
39 Hidalgo house
42 Existed
43 Common abbr.

PUZZLE 87

ACROSS

1 Squashlike fruits
7 Ex of Artie and Mickey
10 Omitted (2 wds.)
11 Dolts
13 "The Towering __"
14 __ Oyl (Popeye's gal)
15 Ott or Brooks
16 Evergreen shrub
17 Antique
18 Purple flower
20 Historical records
21 Singer __ Turner
22 Infant
24 Romantic mood enhancer (2 wds.)
30 Dollars
31 Diva's forte
32 Resells tickets
36 Chats
37 Ask to borrow bucks (2 wds.)
38 Home plate judge
41 Thurs. follower
42 "Just __" (No Doubt song, 2 wds.)
43 Of the seashore
45 Ike's wife
46 Game of chance
47 Clown's nose color
48 Mary-Kate's twin

DOWN

1 Universal
2 Disconnected from Wi-Fi
3 Beehive State tribe
4 "Gilmore Girls" daughter
5 Sand formation
6 Put on board
7 Patriot Ethan
8 "Ta-da!"
9 It's sold near the Tylenol
10 Restricts
11 Pupil covering
12 Fractions of minutes (abbr.)
19 __ Jose
20 Fundamentals
22 Gazzara and Hogan
23 Lime drink
25 Fall from height
26 Badger
27 Soldier who didn't volunteer
28 Book-lined room
29 With little effort
32 Hoax
33 Trademark of George Burns
34 "__ to Kill" (2 wds.)
35 Livid
38 Golden State campus, for short
39 Cattle calls
40 Bridle __
44 Home of the Cardinals (abbr.)

PUZZLE 88

ACROSS

1 FYI relative
4 Play begin-
   ning (2 wds.)
8 Sailor's affir-
   matives
12 Tycoon
   Onassis
13 Remunerates
14 Stretch __
15 William __
   Hearst
17 Police alerts
   (abbr.)
18 Three trios
19 Internet sensa-
   tion
21 __ coat
22 Wasp wounds
24 Not before
26 Interstate sight
27 Challenges
28 David's
   favorite son
30 __ Davidson
   motorcycle
32 Not imaginary
35 Interrogator
36 Plug (2 wds.)
38 Reply (abbr.)
39 Clock sound
41 Drive onward
42 "Finally, the
   week is over!"
   initials
44 Pilot's exper-

tise
46 Take-out
   phrase
   (2 wds.)
47 Swingy tune
48 Hallucino-
   genic drug
   (abbr.)
49 The A of A.D.
50 Missile housing
51 Sib's nickname

DOWN

1 Homes for
   some owls
2 Characteristics
3 "__-the-Pooh"
4 Soldier's
   address letters
5 Makes
   peaceful
6 Sort
7 "Moby-Dick"
   narrator
8 Chicken __
   king (2 wds.)
9 "Yay!"
10 Campfire
   remains
11 Cubs legend
   Sammy
16 "Hamlet" locale
20 Hard work
23 Kind of gravy
25 Break in a
   sporting event

(2 wds.)
27 24 hours
29 Continuing
   tales
30 "__ Sloopy"
   (pop song,
   2 wds.)
31 Appoint
33 Rainy months
34 "Dracula" star
   Bela
36 Competence
37 Remains
   undecided
38 "__ boy!"
40 107, to Nero
43 Egg __ yung
45 From __ Z
   (2 wds.)

PUZZLE 89

ACROSS

1 Alphabet start
6 Stream sediment
10 Emphatic refusal
11 Decisive victory
15 Poise
16 Reestablish
17 Transgresses
18 Singer Cantrell
19 Lucky number, to Nero?
20 Response to an online joke
21 Slangy reply
22 Religious offenses
23 Makes broader
25 Scarlett's beau
26 Roof overhang
27 Suds
28 Spend carelessly
30 Historical marker, often
32 Muscular pain
33 Mideastern country
34 Weekend comedy show, briefly
36 Inventor's monogram
37 "Don't have __!" (Bart Simpson quote, 2 wds.)
38 Frequently baked pasta
39 Treachery
41 Pie nut
42 Shipping
43 Interweave three strands of hair
44 Lip
45 Jovial

DOWN

1 Guardian __
2 Take a loan
3 "Two and a Half Men" actor (2 wds.)
4 Severinsen and Holliday
5 Fleecy one
6 Purse holders
7 Singer Cara
8 Actress Hartman
9 Egyptian boy-king
12 "Grease" or "Cabaret" (2 wds.)
13 Produce books
14 Robbery
18 Solitary
21 Campbell of "Scream"
22 Former Lakers center
24 Calendar number
25 Pony color
27 Diamond value reducer
28 Electrical units
29 Without __ in the world (2 wds.)
30 Antlers' points
31 Demand
33 Church pictures
35 __ hop (jitterbug variation)
37 Hong Kong's continent
38 Coke __ (diet soft drink)
40 Magazine inserts
41 Lunchbox sandwich, for short

PUZZLE 90

ACROSS

1 Large nail
6 Spoil (2 wds.)
11 Form a queue (2 wds.)
13 An Astaire
14 Communion tables
15 Projector parts
16 Capital of Switzerland
17 Nonchoosy one's word
19 Highways (abbr.)
21 Michael or Mike
23 Crux
24 Ambulance worker (abbr.)
25 Thomas __ Edison
26 Solstice cele- brators
30 Anger
32 Excellent aviators
33 Rep.'s opponent
34 "Look __ Talking"
35 Inhabitant
39 iPhone assist- ant
40 "Notes __ Scandal" (2006 film, 2 wds.)

41 "Terrible" czar
43 Incite (2 wds.)
45 Struck by Cupid's arrow (2 wds.)
47 "__ I Don't Have You"
48 Athlete's "closet"
49 Delicious
50 Mantel, e.g.

DOWN

1 Thick piece
2 Stacked
3 Preface to a book, for short
4 Reeves of "The Matrix"
5 Asia's neighbor (abbr.)
6 Cooper et al.
7 "__ to a Night- ingale"
8 Part of a six- pack (2 wds.)
9 In sum (2 wds.)
10 Be entitled to
12 Biblical hymns
18 Crooner "King" Cole
20 Burn
22 Patton, for one (abbr.)
26 Handles roughly
27 Most sore
28 Atlanta's locale
29 Delegates
30 Small item
31 Parisian pal
33 Continuous noise
35 __ Island, New York
36 Nothing
37 Bring forth
38 __ orange
42 Foamy football
44 Trick or treat mo.
46 Thumbs-down votes

PUZZLE 91

ACROSS

1 Travel on foot
6 Floats
12 Detecting device
13 Not as difficult
14 Former "Today" host Couric
15 Farm implements of yore
16 Sitter
18 Brit. VIPs
19 Location
20 Army rank (abbr.)
23 Fastens
27 Brummell or Bridges
28 Pacific paradise
29 Mom, e.g.
31 __ hygiene
32 Silent Cal __
34 Fabray, for short
35 Soggy areas
36 Alphabetic trio
39 Art class creation
42 Sailor's emphatic reply (2 wds.)
44 Open, as a flower
46 Tricks
47 Transplant
48 Tax return reviews
49 Helpers (abbr.)

DOWN

1 "What a shame!"
2 Gad about
3 Freeze start
4 Mast attachment
5 Foretell
6 Official edict
7 Crowd's cheer
8 "Your time __!" (2 wds.)
9 Like some mattresses
10 Type of bike (2 wds.)
11 Last-year students (abbr.)
17 Guiding principle
21 Vampire's tooth
22 Pleasingly pretty
23 "This suitcase weighs __!" (2 wds.)
24 Reid or Lipinski
25 Merci (2 wds.)
26 Ghost
27 Hairbrush components
30 High school math
33 Be preoccupied with
37 Go first
38 Long skirt
40 Law officers
41 Call of derision
42 "Gotcha!"
43 So far
45 Sinai and Olympus (abbr.)

PUZZLE 92

ACROSS

1 Medical subj.
5 Confirms attendance
10 Cartoon from Japan
11 Expects
13 Hunting dog (2 wds.)
15 Itinerary info (abbr.)
16 Piece of the pie
17 Quick to learn
18 Jazz's Fitz-gerald
20 Immediately (abbr.)
21 Govt. agcy.
22 Business bigwigs (abbr.)
23 Tenement area
25 Trestle support
27 Explorer __ de Leon
31 Trim
34 Close tightly
35 Letters on some SUVs
38 Colt's mom
40 Letter opener
41 Sound from the hot tub
42 Syrian's neighbor
44 A.M. show, briefly
45 Hold nothing back (3 wds.)

48 "Got Milk?," e.g.
49 Ski resort
50 Those with ESP
51 Laundry amount

DOWN

1 Memoirist Maya
2 Naught
3 French friends
4 Electric auto
5 Mischievous one
6 Use a broom, say (2 wds.)
7 Witch's cauldron
8 Pocket breads
9 "The Thirty-Nine __" (Hitchcock)
10 Doe's lack
12 Mexico City miss (abbr.)
13 Build
14 Radiator sound
19 Org.
24 Lichen
26 Study group
28 Spoke like steeds
29 Electra of "Scary Movie"

films
30 Martinelli et al.
32 Copland and Spelling
33 Ensnare
35 Orthodontist's challenges
36 Handles roughly
37 Sevigny of "Boys Don't Cry"
39 Fifty-fifty
43 "You're __ much trouble!" (2 wds.)
46 Bigger than med.
47 April 15th fig.

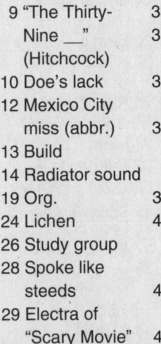

PUZZLE 93

ACROSS

1 "__ Bovary"
7 Illuminated (2 wds.)
12 Yearly
13 "That's __ how-do-you-do!" (2 wds.)
14 Evening gown material
15 Rest stop sights
16 Loaf variety
17 Address book abbr.
18 Take care of (2 wds.)
19 "__ forgiven"
21 Winter complaints
22 Beef cut
23 Horse's metalwear
25 Rodeo challenge (2 wds.)
31 Pads
32 Cut grain
33 The __ Family Singers
36 Critic Roger
37 At that locale
38 Long-running comedy show (abbr.)
40 Barely

passing grade
41 "Extra Dry" deodorant
42 Added up
44 Say "up and at 'em!"
45 Secret newlywed
46 Had
47 Stately homes

DOWN

1 Girl Ricky Nelson said "hello" to (2 wds.)
2 Like a cherub
3 Genetic letters
4 Mom's sisters
5 Activity book

favorite
6 Israeli carrier (2 wds.)
7 Dogie roper
8 "Man! __ Like a Woman!" (Shania Twain, 2 wds.)
9 Measured in minutes
10 Definite quantities
11 Mexican money
14 Toothbrush type (hyph.)
20 Calligrapher's purchase
21 Corn ears
23 Finger noise
24 Elevation measure (abbr.)
26 Hindered
27 Globe
28 One who pesters
29 Professions
30 Elected
33 Toss
34 Show again
35 Begin a revolt
36 Rocker __ John
37 Poi source
38 Leaf support
39 1916 Lopez hit
43 Soldier's address (abbr.)

PUZZLE 94

ACROSS

1 Trick
6 Swarm
10 Courageous TV collie
12 "__ living" (2 wds.)
13 Carried out orders
14 Main idea
16 Vowed
17 GI's missile
19 Vintage auto
20 Bedlam
22 Twinings product
23 Approximation phrase (2 wds.)
25 Disagreement
27 Smoker's remains
29 __ tree (cornered, 2 wds.)
30 Become less
34 "Waterloo" group
38 Dental gp.
39 Opted for
41 Mess up
42 Type of "reality"
44 AKA C-sharp (hyph.)
46 Anesthetic, once
47 Invest with ministerial duty
49 Golfer's target
50 Dirtied
51 Moved swiftly
52 Drops of sweat

DOWN

1 Less rapid
2 Forbidden things
3 Manipulator
4 Group that featured Justin Timberlake
5 Neckwear
6 "Pencils down!" (2 wds.)
7 Collar style
8 Millionaire's home
9 Winless racehorse
11 Candice Bergen's father
15 Deed
16 Box office sign (abbr.)
18 Rascals
21 Sounds of laughter (3 wds.)
24 Rowing tool
26 Goat's sound
28 Reinforced
30 Brubeck of jazz
31 Bunker et al.
32 Waitress on skates
33 Single performances
35 Contradicted
36 Kleenex, Colgate, Campbell's, etc.
37 Illustrations
40 Jockey Arcaro
43 Prefix for gram or port
45 FDR's dog
48 Director Reiner

ACROSS

1 "Modern Family" role
4 Former baseball manager Felipe
8 Some pickles
10 Cut short
13 Octopus's home
14 Watch carefully
15 Pro votes
16 Purchase
17 Nays
18 Absent
19 Hula hoop twirlers
20 Toil
21 Posh
23 Chicago, for one
24 Mined find
25 Prone to misbehaving
26 Alphabetic quartet
28 Exercises (2 wds.)
32 Challenge
33 Takes a chair
34 Compass heading
35 Taxi alternative
36 "Who cares?"
37 Revise proofs
38 Pullman train
40 Make joyful
41 Canines' quarters
42 Long walks
43 Doctor's "pronto!"
44 Moses parted one

DOWN

1 Traction aids for athletes
2 Plaintive cry
3 Hotmail provider (abbr.)
4 Roast beef fast food chain
5 __ Angeles
6 Dentist's request (2 wds.)
7 Remove forcibly
8 "__ Want to Dance?" (2 wds.)
9 Become frosty (2 wds.)
10 Automobile type
11 100%
12 Student's study surface
16 Peevishness
19 Spy Mata __
22 Understandable
23 Campbell's Soup containers
25 The two
26 Aesop's story
27 Salad ingredients
28 Wedding cake layers
29 Songwriter Neil
30 Join as one
31 Sampras and Seeger
32 Early evening
33 Salmon's relative
37 Writer Wiesel
39 Garden vegetable
40 Sounds of inquiry

PUZZLE 96

ACROSS

1 Says further
5 River transport
9 Tut's title
12 Charles Lamb's pen name
13 Canadian "state"
14 Maladies
15 Gathered leaves
16 Pea, e.g.
18 March date
19 Sieve
21 Author Talese
22 Rocker Bon Jovi
23 Positioned a golf ball
24 Had a crush on, to a Brit
26 Actor James __
28 Large vase
29 Throng
32 "Hmmmm" (3 wds.)
34 Long, mournful cry
35 Whole thing
36 Military cap
37 Straight __ arrow (2 wds.)
38 Storytellers
41 Dark reddish brown
42 Spiny sea creatures
43 Expresses disapproval
44 Writing tablets

DOWN

1 Like Arizona's climate
2 Dapper guy
3 Physician, slangily
4 Bombard
5 Ruled, as a queen
6 Reference indirectly
7 Shot a movie
8 Stun gun
9 "The Devil Wears __" (2003 bestseller)
10 "The __ Pokey" (kids' song)
11 Broad roads (abbr.)
13 Fussbudget
17 Consumed
19 Swindle
20 As expected (2 wds.)
22 A Lennon Sister
24 Food shortages
25 Vexation
26 National headcount
27 Assault
29 Nitwit
30 People with debts
31 Certain sandwiches
32 Jumped
33 Waffle topping
34 Mythical monster
36 Scrooge's words
39 Memorable time
40 Calculator display (abbr.)

PUZZLE 97

ACROSS

1 Garbed
5 Tennis's Shriver
8 San ___ Padres
9 Chevy model
12 Giants great (2 wds.)
13 Humiliates
14 In the twinkling ___ eye (2 wds.)
15 Soak
17 Nervous
19 Franklin's flier
20 Bonnet
21 Ladies of Spain (abbr.)
23 Society miss
26 Skunk feature
28 Boulders
31 Male descendant
32 Former mlles.
34 Dover's state (abbr.)
35 Move ever so slightly
37 Singer Page
39 Names to a position
43 Ointment
44 Berated
45 Spheres
47 Steamships
48 Hammer and wrench
49 Assoc.
50 Personal welfare

DOWN

1 Salsa herb
2 Jaworski and Spinks
3 Actor's rep.
4 Gumdrop brand
5 Leaning Tower city
6 Urge on
7 Inspiring one
8 Conquers
9 "La Danse" painter Henri
10 Adjoin
11 "Streets of ___"
12 Sweater pests
16 Alias inits.
18 Psychic letters
22 Brings to memory
24 It goes next to the couch (2 wds.)
25 Ladybugs, e.g.
27 Sneaker part
29 Cooking measure (abbr.)
30 Becomes slender
33 Bejeweled "A-Team" member (2 wds.)
36 Layer
38 "You can't judge ___..." (2 wds.)
39 Singer ___ Guthrie
40 Au ___ (nanny)
41 Ricochet sound
42 Cpls.' superiors (abbr.)
46 Mauna ___

PUZZLE 98

ACROSS

1 War club
5 Wednesday's father
10 Sufficient
12 Intention
14 Long
15 Not included
16 Organization (abbr.)
17 Suburban barbecue locale
18 Ox joiner
20 Work force
23 Candidate Landon
26 Implusive
28 Verdi opera
29 Noisy dog
31 Ready (2 wds.)
33 Steady
34 53, to Nero
36 "Major Crimes" network
37 Relieve tension
38 Rugged rock
40 Johanna Spyri book
43 Unadorned
47 Liken
49 Andes beast
50 Less soiled
51 "__ Joe's" (2 wds.)
52 Grants temporarily
53 Legislators (abbr.)

DOWN

1 Poet Angelou
2 Singer Ed __
3 Accountants (abbr.)
4 "The Jetsons" son
5 Rough particles
6 Pertaining to vision
7 Driver
8 Japan or Taiwan follower
9 Last English letter
11 Theater cry
12 Catholic Church heads
13 Actress Thurman of "Pulp Fiction"
19 Marx or Malden
21 Eve's home
22 Electrical unit
23 Busy as __ (2 wds.)
24 Volcanic matter
25 High school newcomers
27 __ trigger
30 Skateboarder's protection
32 Responsible
35 Colder
39 Grand festivals
41 Hunter et al.
42 Rapper Dr. __
44 Satisfy
45 Somali supermodel
46 Popular pets
47 250, to Cicero
48 Bullring "rah"

PUZZLE 99

ACROSS

1 Cager Thurmond et al.
6 A Great Lake
10 Olympian Jesse
11 Conspicuous
14 Fasten again
15 One who changes
16 Like Ivory Soap
17 Small guitars, informally
18 FDR program (abbr.)
19 Birthday number
20 Plain bird
21 Impose a tax
22 Toyota's Prius, e.g.
24 Opposing teams
25 Argument
27 Turn out
30 Overtly
33 "Taken" star Neeson
34 "Whoa!"
35 Lout
37 Accent ingredient
38 Cinematic sleuth Charlie
39 ___ fide
40 Hit's box office sign (2 wds.)
42 Tries to get a tan
43 PGA pro Lee
44 Naval group
45 Sardine holders
46 Speeders' penalties

DOWN

1 Actress Shearer
2 "Anchors ___"
3 Lipton rival
4 Author Bagnold
5 Compass letters
6 Actress Burstyn
7 Disloyal associates
8 Suffix for suburban or meteor
9 Made money
11 Oven-roasted spud (2 wds.)
12 Temerity
13 Carhops' props
17 Author Leon ("Trinity")
20 Legal paper
21 Property attachment
23 Sleeping qtrs.
24 Dance movement
26 Current with (2 wds.)
27 Horror film locale (2 wds., abbr.)
28 Helmet opening
29 Aerie occupant
31 Slacken
32 "___ Doodle Dandy"
34 Snubs
36 Goes hungry
38 Invent, as a phrase
39 Island near Java
41 506, Roman-style
42 Close chum, to a texter

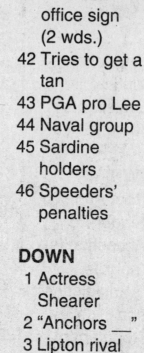

PUZZLE 100

ACROSS

1 Undamaged
7 Papa's mama, to some
11 Deep sadness
12 Objects of worship
14 Blood condition
15 France's Antoinette
16 They're confessed at confession
17 David __ Stiers
18 Shortly, informally (3 wds.)
21 Sailor's affirmatives
22 Change again
24 Boxing verdict (abbr.)
27 Food brand for Fido
28 Grown puppy
29 Work force
30 __ Lanka
31 All of us
33 Split asunder
36 Matthau's frequent costar
37 Panic
39 "Pequod" captain
40 Macaroni shape
41 Royal abode
44 Actor Cornel
45 Ring bearer's prop
46 Jury member
47 Secret meetings

DOWN

1 "...__ penny earned" (2 wds.)
2 The opposite of "oui"
3 Rapunzel's glory
4 Military groups
5 Occurred
6 simultaneously
6 "__ the night before..."
7 Leonard of "Star Trek"
8 Axiom
9 __ Rack (department store)
10 "__ of the Mind" (2 wds.)
13 Certain elected official (abbr.)
18 Eye part
19 Come close
20 Worthy of respect
21 Delicate pasta
23 State VIP (abbr.)
25 Atlantic City game
26 "Closer" actor Clive
29 Band's round, brass clashers
32 Actually
34 Wear away
35 Later
37 Use thread
38 Curl holder
39 Calendar jotting (abbr.)
42 Sleeping spot
43 Grossed-out sounds

PUZZLE 101

ACROSS
1 Croc's kin
6 "What happens in ___..."
11 Deceive
12 Dublin denizens
13 Some Spanish speakers
14 To the point
15 Just get by
16 Caribbean resort island
18 Golf great Trevino
19 Ruling body (abbr.)
21 Bridge coup
22 Liner (abbr.)
23 Kettle product
25 Math course
27 Chips in
29 Intrusive one
32 Actor Baldwin
34 "Cheers" waitress
36 Channel that shows musical videos (abbr.)
39 Actor Sharif
41 Telephone face, once
42 Wide loafer width
43 Golf course chunk
45 Problem for TV's Monk (abbr.)
46 "___ beaucoup!"
48 Hamlet's love
50 Weight measurement
51 Showed dizziness
52 Eyeglasses, for short
53 British streetcars

DOWN
1 Revenge oneself (2 wds.)
2 "The Greatest" boxer
3 Casserole ingredient
4 What Glade covers
5 Aftermath
6 Nutrient in citrus fruit (2 wds.)
7 Prior, in poetry
8 HBO series
9 Valuable
10 Like chiffon
11 South ___ (The Coyote State)
13 Mobster Diamond
17 Gin joints
20 "Cheerio!" (2 wds.)
24 "Merrie ___" (cartoons)
26 Urge on
28 Tractor-trailer
30 Baltimore baseball team
31 Lake ___, N.Y.
33 Caper
35 "M*A*S*H" star
36 Inbox items
37 Prepare to drive (2 wds.)
38 Author Jules
40 Lassoer
44 "Take ___ Train" (2 wds.)
47 300, to Cicero
49 Dutch disease

PUZZLE 102

ACROSS

1 Holey cheese
6 Bacterium
10 Seek
11 Bottled water brand
13 Fox trot, e.g. (2 wds.)
15 Spirited tune
16 Pursues ardently
17 __ Paulo, Brazil
18 Gone by
19 Height (abbr.)
20 Stitched together
21 Until now (2 wds.)
23 Frisbee, for one
25 Wrap around
27 Installs
31 Deborah or Jean
33 Alert
34 Preston and Bilko (abbr.)
37 Goals
39 Chicken __ (childhood disease)
40 Comic strip word
41 Prima donna
42 French miss (abbr.)
43 Be kept waiting (3 wds.)
46 All in __ work (2 wds.)
47 Cuts of meat
48 Captain Hook's henchman
49 Karenina et al.

DOWN

1 Liquidate, as stocks (2 wds.)
2 "Pogo" creator Kelly
3 Abbr. on a clearance tag
4 Threatening expression
5 Yelled "scat!"
6 Some diplomas (abbr.)
7 Zsa Zsa's sister
8 Washing cycle
9 Colorful parrot with a giant beak
10 Former capital of South Vietnam
12 Broadway light
13 Unenthused
14 Cinema
19 Writer Gardner
20 Distort
22 Astronauts' approvals (hyph.)
24 Married
women in Madrid (abbr.)
26 Use a colander
28 Some pills
29 Gnomes
30 Male and female
32 Actress Chita
34 Animal rights org.
35 Products
36 Early morning hour (2 wds., abbr.)
38 "Perry __"
41 Rx notation
42 Arizona city
44 Caustic substance
45 Leia's "Star Wars" hero

PUZZLE 103

ACROSS

1 College student's concern (abbr.)
4 Poor community
8 Sharply inclined
10 Winter apple
14 Opera solos
15 Bric-a-brac holder
16 Delude
18 Ranter
19 Dashboard abbr.
20 Coal vein
22 __ crow
23 Calendar's span
25 Advanced medical students
27 Byrd's rank (abbr.)
29 Football coups (abbr.)
30 Kind of pudding
33 Pinball error
37 Raincoat, for short
38 107, to Caesar
39 Boston cream __
40 Red as __ (2 wds.)
42 Grinds
45 "Arabian Nights" hero (2 wds.)
47 Use a gun
48 Ted Kennedy, e.g.
49 Bright
50 Words of agreement, out West
51 TX to NY dir.

DOWN

1 Far East hostess
2 Ring
3 Part of a church
4 Norway neighbor
5 Eng. course
6 Weaponless
7 Bucks or ton start
8 Slugger Sosa
9 Trivial matter
11 Deadly Sins number
12 Regions
13 Sprightly
17 Classic sci-fi author
21 Reach
24 MTV genre, often
26 Letters after Q
28 Call the shots
30 __ of contents
31 __ the hole (2 wds.)
32 Panatelas
34 Apple product
35 __ the stand (commit perjury, 2 wds.)
36 Snappish
37 Pasture sounds
41 Internet auction site
43 Part of AARP (abbr.)
44 Evade
46 Type of jazz

PUZZLE 104

ACROSS

1 Chips in
6 Group of aides
11 Lebanon's neighbor
12 Loiter
13 Blemish on a loafer
14 Wore away
15 Musician's deg.
16 Casualties
17 Candy cane's flavor
21 Tankard filler
22 52, Roman-style
23 Transmission parts
27 Gone by
29 "My Gal __"
31 Ballet exercise
32 Hawaii's "hello"
34 Encountered
36 Sleeve card
37 Farmer's water management
40 Actress Bynes
43 Mamie's man
44 Houston athlete
45 Necklace items
48 Gracie and Ethan
49 Legal
50 Say without thinking
51 Mrs. Mertz

DOWN

1 Hee-hawer on the farm
2 Columbia's locale (abbr.)
3 High card in bridge
4 Paris's __ Tower
5 Jungle trips
6 Tahitian skirt
7 Ballroom dance (hyph.)
8 Does sums
9 Run away
10 FBI agents, for short
12 Lox location
17 Dad
18 Flier to Tel Aviv (2 wds.)
19 South of the border money
20 Home of the Dolphins
24 Jai __
25 Edward G. Robinson role
26 Spotted
28 Ponderer
30 Easy to read
33 Fervent
35 __ on the lam (2 wds.)
38 Long-tailed rodents
39 Impart knowledge
40 Middle Easterner
41 "__ Flanders"
42 Rights advocacy org.
46 "__ Hard"
47 Home of the Cardinals (abbr.)

PUZZLE 105

ACROSS

1 Energy measures (abbr.)
5 Federal tax agcy.
8 Join together
9 Bruins' gp.
10 Body art, for short
14 Trial figure (abbr.)
15 What the rat became in "Cinderella"
17 Sinbad, e.g.
19 Colorado city
20 Approached stealthily
22 Expert with mosaics
23 Intertwine the hair
25 Russo of "Outbreak"
26 Consists of
29 Invite over the threshold (2 wds.)
31 Sesame and Wall (abbr.)
32 Showing, as a rerun (2 wds.)
34 Causing chills
36 Song part
38 Summon (2 wds.)
42 Uncertainties
44 Chevy model
45 Modern communications medium
47 Korbut of gymnastics
48 __ Trueheart
49 Southwestern tribe
50 Duke's st.
51 Trio after A
52 College VIPs

DOWN

1 Couturier Bill __
2 Gigantic person
3 Undo sneakers
4 First U.S. space station
5 Enlarge
6 Frat letter
7 Strike smartly
10 "A League of __ Own"
11 Strolls
12 __ agent (Hollywood figure)
13 Night noises
16 A __ above the rest
18 Gumbo pods
21 Flood blockers
24 Worked on a movie set
26 "Stop where you are!" (2 wds.)
27 Whichever person
28 Swaggers
30 1492 ship
33 Strange feelings
35 O'Brien of "D.O.A."
37 Middle (abbr.)
39 Edie of "Nurse Jackie"
40 Stadium music maker
41 Bellows
43 Ignore purposely
46 Abbr. after a list

PUZZLE 106

ACROSS

1 Cloudless
6 Singer Mama __
10 Clock indicators
11 Acts like a sponge
15 Magic Kingdom's neighbor
16 Dries up (2 wds.)
17 Pig's pad
18 Refs' kin
20 Start of a magical phrase
21 Anklet
23 Prepared to golf
25 Heart test (abbr.)
26 Supple
28 Monsters
30 Nighttime hunters
31 Wrongful act, legally
32 Arizona natives
34 Group of war vessels
36 Lone
37 Neighbor of Tex.
39 Longings
41 Chauffeur's offering
43 Manhattan cops gp.
45 Tennis necessity
46 Crocheted mats
48 Japanese cartoon art
50 Empowers
51 Shroud of __
52 "...__ good night" (2 wds.)
53 Exxon rival

DOWN

1 Kind of board
2 Easy-to-tote computer
3 Reference work in several volumes
4 Confused bustle
5 Q followers
6 Floor furnishing
7 Maltreat
8 9-digit ID (abbr.)
9 "Slamming Sammy"
12 "Raging Bull" actor (3 wds.)
13 Actress Delta
14 Male deer
19 Range components (abbr.)
22 Tropical fruit
24 Gloom's partner
27 Part of AKA
29 Dull color
31 Booby __
32 Vast crowd
33 __ soup
34 Milano of "Charmed"
35 Low in iron
38 Begin to garden, perhaps
40 __ pool
42 Exile locale
44 Factual information
47 "__ drink to that!"
49 Book before Deut.

PUZZLE 107

ACROSS

1 Tour leaders
7 Lion's neck hair
11 Gets under one's skin
12 Disgraced
14 Feels for
15 Donkey in Milne books
16 Fifty-fifty
17 Wisconsin city
18 Sun. speech
19 Growing older
21 Cottontail
23 All __ (attentive)
27 Explorer
28 Pitched
29 Prince William's alma mater
30 "Sophie's __"
31 Clear a window
33 Cut down
35 TV's "__ Med"
39 Treaty org.
40 Chinese brew
41 Trap setter
43 Items sent to the laundry
44 Governs
45 Pigeon-__
46 Most competent

DOWN

1 Hangs open
2 Cosmos
3 Be outgoing
4 Exhaust (2 wds.)
5 __ shadow
6 Snake's sound
7 Polite request (2 wds.)
8 "Famous" cookie maker
9 Roman fiddler
10 Biblical locale
12 Combs or Astin
13 Video games' Sonic
17 Major engineering school (abbr.)
19 More than enough
20 Beat it, cowboy-style
22 Halloween shout
24 Onassis, for short
25 Restore a battery
26 Adds sugar
28 Still, to a poet
30 Corporate bigwig (abbr.)
32 Hennery products
34 Poorest
35 __ of living
36 Part of Santa's laugh (2 wds.)
37 Tennis's Nastase
38 Extension __
39 Carpentry need
41 Mme., in Madrid
42 Neighbor of Wyo.

PUZZLE 108

ACROSS

1 Polar feature
7 Saying
12 Barber of Seville's name
13 Winter beverage
14 Squalls
15 Pitches
16 "__ creature was stirring..." (2 wds.)
18 Physique
19 Eye surgery beam
22 Light wood
24 "Now __ me down to sleep" (2 wds.)
25 Football official
28 Convened
29 Fuses metals
30 Hebrew priest
31 Buzzing abodes
33 Sword handle
34 Register (2 wds.)
35 "The Bells of St. __"
36 Counterfeit coin
37 Emerald Isle
39 Supermarket path
41 Snub
45 Beef animal
46 Sunglasses, slangily
47 Gossip's Hopper
48 Lucy's pal et al.

DOWN

1 Conditional words
2 Young camp worker (abbr.)
3 Personality
4 Gleason's "Honeymooners" costar
5 Suit for Lancelot
6 Hitching __
7 Disgusted German cry
8 Tennis grouping
9 Crossword heading
10 Former Israeli PM (2 wds.)
11 "__ does it!"
17 Kansas city
19 Tree branch
20 Sheltered, asea
21 Moon, e.g.
23 Connecting words
25 Son of Leah
26 Treaty associate
27 Insect young
29 Moved like a happy puppy
32 Gave accommodations
33 Mother of Samuel
35 Could possibly
36 Miss America accessory
38 Float like a balloon
40 Epoch
42 Poem of praise
43 Family tree branch (abbr.)
44 Lisper's challenge

PUZZLE 1

```
  F A I T H     F I R M
P E R S U A D E   A S E A
R E L A T I O N   T R A Y
O L E   U R N S     A P O
V E N D   S T U   L E E R
O R E O S   B E H O L D S
      M O D E S T Y
A N G E L I C   S A L S A
L A O S   M R S   L A P S
I M A   P U T A   S R O
B A T S   L E A V E S I N
I T E M   E L B O W I N G
S H E S       S W E E T
```

PUZZLE 2

```
  P L A S M A     A L G
  H E C T I C   M E D I A
  A G H A S T   A M E N S
A R I   I T S   Z I P U P
C A B I N     D O N T S
C O L D   A M I L E
T H E L O N E R A N G E R
    E D N A S   C A N E
  S A N D S   S E R T A
T H R E E   A L E   B E D
S E U S S   C A V I A R
P A B S T   E M E R G E
S R A     D A R K E R
```

PUZZLE 3

```
  B D R M   C L A W
C O O E D   A E R O B I C
H O L D S   R E F R E S H
A N T E   A P R   D E L I
D E S E R V E   S P A M
    M O R T A L   E N E
A A A   M I C R O   D D S
T L C   E L L E N S
T I C S   E N G A G E D
I B E T   B A A   F A L A
L I N E M A N   S A T O N
A S T A I R E   P R E P S
    L I A R   R I D E
```

PUZZLE 4

```
P A G E R   B A R B R A
A L E X A   A L R E A D Y
C O L I N   M I S S I V E
T E S T T U B E   I N S T
          S I N G E
A F F O R D   A G I L E
T R I V I A   S L E I G H
M O R A L   L A D I E S
      L L A M A
D E P T   H O G W A R T S
L Y R I C A L   E V E R Y
I R O N O R E   R I P E N
  E M E N D S   E V O K E
```

PUZZLE 5

```
  L I M P S   T H U M B
C A M A R O   R I G O R
A B A S E D   E T H N I C
S E C T S   L A S S O E R
A L S O   L E T   C F O
    D L I I   M A L E S
A C C O S T   E L D E R S
B L O N D   R E B A
Y O U   J F K   P R A M
S T R O K E D   A T I M E
S T A K E S   O L I V I A
  E G R E T   R O N A L D
D E A N S   B U G L E
```

PUZZLE 6

```
S C O R N   H E A T
K A Z O O   M O T H E R
A L A M B   O N T I M E
T O R P I D   S I G M A
P E R K   G O P   C H A R
A R I   A D M I T S
S S E   D E I C E   T B A
    I V A N K A   R I M
S O L O   L G E   D I S C
A V O W S   O D D E S T
R E S A L E   O I L E R
A R E N A S   F A L C O
  R S V P   F L A T S
```

PUZZLE 7

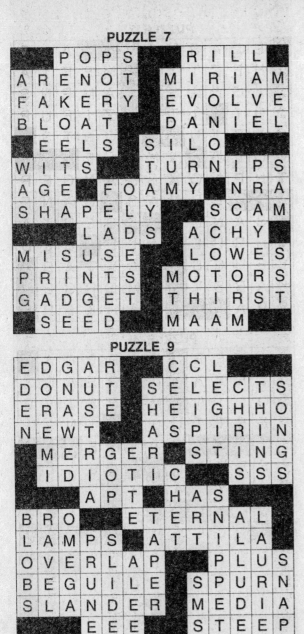

```
P O P S       R I L L
A R E N O T   M I R I A M
F A K E R Y   E V O L V E
B L O A T     D A N I E L
  E E L S   S I L O
W I T S     T U R N I P S
A G E   F O A M Y   N R A
S H A P E L Y     S C A M
    L A D S     A C H Y
M I S U S E     L O W E S
P R I N T S   M O T O R S
G A D G E T   T H I R S T
  S E E D     M A A M
```

PUZZLE 8

```
  T O P I C   S Y R U P
T H I R T Y   H A I K U
H O L Y S C R I P T U R E
E R E   A L I E   E L S A
A N D S   O G R E   E U R
      I M P S   T A L E S
  B E Z O S   P O R E S
A R C E D   S A N E
T A U   E S P Y   A I D A
O V A L   P U M A   S O P
M E D I C I N E B A L L S
  S O L A R   N E G A T E
  T R Y T O   T E E M S
```

PUZZLE 9

```
E D G A R     C C L
D O N U T   S E L E C T S
E R A S E   H E I G H H O
N E W T     A S P I R I N
  M E R G E R   S T I N G
  I D I O T I C   S S S
    A P T   H A S
B R O     E T E R N A L
L A M P S   A T T I L A
O V E R L A P   P L U S
B E G U I L E   S P U R N
S L A N D E R   M E D I A
    E E E     S T E E P
```

PUZZLE 10

```
  T A S E R   G O R E S
C A S T R O   I N E R T
A P O L L O P R O G R A M
K E N   E T A L   S A T E
E D G E   I L S A   T U T
    V A N E   A R I E S
  S L A N G   C R O C S
H O I S T   S A P S
A F B   S N U B   S H A M
S T E M   E N O S   E L I
H E R E W E G O A G A I N
  N A M E D   S I E V E S
  S L O B S   E L L E N
```

PUZZLE 11

```
  S T A Y     C A R T E
A D M I R A L   T W I R L
C R I N K L E   R E B U S
C O L E   I T L L   B E A
T O E   V E T O   M O S S
S P R E E   U R G E N T
    D E S C E N D
  M A G P I E   A S C O T
G A R Y   F L O W   H U R
O D E   S T E P   N O T A
M A Y I M   A T T I R E D
E M O T E   F E A T U R E
R E U S E   D E E S
```

PUZZLE 12

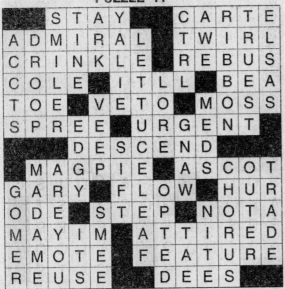

```
      A V E R   O R C A
O H S   R I D E   H E A R
M E M O R I A L   B A M A
A R O W   I M A L O S E R
H O K E Y   T O Y O T A
A N Y   A G A I N   N O T
      N E R V E
A P P   K N E E L   A K A
V I O L E T   Y O D E L
I S R A E L I S   A L A I
A T T N   E R U P T I N G
T O A D   S I L T   B U N
E L L S   T S K S
```

PUZZLE 13

```
A L A S   A G C Y   E R A
L A R A   N I L E   N O S
F U E L   T O U R I S T S
I N T L   O R E   L I T E
E C H O I N G   I G E T
  H A W A I I   B E N D S
    G O O S E
R A M B O   A T E A S E
E V E L   R A T T A N S
L E N O   A M P   R U T H
O R I G I N A L   E C R U
A S A   D A N E   S E A T
D E L   S T I R   T S P S
```

PUZZLE 14

```
  A H A S   H E R B S
C L A M P S   A T E A M
H E Y Y O U   R A N C I D
A X E   T B S P   O K L A
N A S A   U H O H   L I V
    D A R E   O Z O N E
S C R A M B L E D E G G S
C R I M E   T E S S
O O P   S U E R   T A G S
T A T A   P R I G   B O A
S K I L L S   E M B A R K
  E D D I E   R E E S E S
  D E A L T   N E E D
```

PUZZLE 15

```
H A H A   S P A M
O R A L B   S C A R A B S
S E R T A   N E C K T I E
E N D   T H I N   S H A W
S A O   T A T E   E S E
    F A L L   E L M E R
  C H I E F   P L E A D
N O E L S   R O O T
I M A   C L I P   I V E
N E R O   L A M E   C O B
J O I N S U P   R A I D S
A N N O Y E D   S T A K E
  G R R S   O N A N
```

PUZZLE 16

```
A D A P T S   S T A G
M O B H I T   C A P E R
C H R O M E   U P P E D
  I B E T   B I L K S
A C I D I C   D A N A
B U N G A L O W   U P A
E L S E   O N E   A D E S
S T P   C A L M N E S S
  E W O K   L O N D O N
M O C H A   L U R E
A N T I S   A P A T H Y
S T O L E   B O L T E D
  O R E S   S N E E R S
```

PUZZLE 17

```
  S H E S   M I C A
  S H O N E   S T A G E
C L A R E T   N E V A D A
O A K S   B I B   S I G H
M M E   L A N C E   N E O
O S T R I C H   L E A R Y
  H A N K A A R O N
A L I F E   B L O N D E R
V I N   D A I L Y   A V E
O L G A   G T O   T G I F
N A S C A R   F L O A T S
  C U R S E   M A R I A
  P E P E   E V E N
```

PUZZLE 18

```
M A K E M E   R A T E D
P R E T A X   O N K E Y
G E N E R A L S T O R E
  S T R   C I I I
    N O T M E   D O D O
S M E A R   A R R I V E S
P I L L S   O N E A L
A T A L O S S   C O N D O
R E L Y   W A L K S
    M E N U   A C E
T H E O D D C O U P L E
O B E S E   A F R A I D
M O L T S   S A S S E S
```

PUZZLE 19

```
S A G A . . . . I S S O .
. T R A M P S . S P O T S
B A R B A R A . A L P H A
A L I . S E L F . A H E M
L E V . S P A R E T I R E
M R E D . . D E L T A S .
. . . E K G . E K E . . .
. A P P E A L . . R A H S
A N A L Y Z I N G . L E E
V I C E . A N O N . L A X
O M I T S . . D R A P E R Y
W A N E S . A A R O N S .
. L O D E . . . L E S T .
```

PUZZLE 20

```
Y W C A . A P T T O . . .
O R E O . F R I E N D S .
H A N K . L I N E S O U T
O P T S . A M Y S . N E V
H U E . S T E T . S O D A
O P R A H . D I L U T E D
. . . N I T . M E L . . .
O C O N N O R . A K R O N
M O N A . D A R N . A L E
A M I . E D G E . A L D A
R E C Y C L E S . S P I T
. S E E H E R E . T H E E
. . W O R S T . A S S N .
```

PUZZLE 21

```
. B L O B . . T U L S A .
. L A U R A . A N E M I A
P A T R O L . L O N E R S
E M T . A M O K . A A R P
W E E K D A Y S . R A E .
. . H W Y S . A C E I N .
. N C A A . . B A R D . .
C O R N Y . G I R L . . .
L O A . C A D I L L A C .
E D Y S . A P E D . I N D
F L O O R S . A G E N T S
S E L F I E . L E V E E .
. S A T B Y . D A N S . .
```

PUZZLE 22

```
. I O N S . T H U M B S .
E D N A S . H A R P O N .
C R E P T . R I G H T E D
R I D E . B O R E . T E E
U S O . S L A Y . D O Z E
. L E T I T . M I M E D .
S L E E P . S E A L S . .
S C A L P . C R A Z E . .
E R R S . G O A D . S I R
N O B . B E N S . R S T U
T O I L I N G . P A P A S
. G L O R I A . A G I L E
. E L U D E S . D U T Y .
```

PUZZLE 23

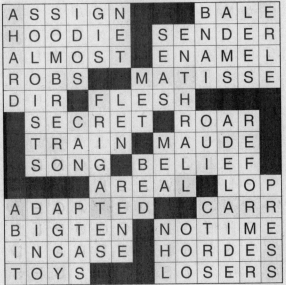

```
A S S I G N . . B A L E .
H O O D I E . S E N D E R
A L M O S T . E N A M E L
R O B S . M A T I S S E .
D I R . F L E S H . . . .
. S E C R E T . R O A R .
. T R A I N . M A U D E .
. S O N G . B E L I E F .
. . A R E A L . L O P . .
A D A P T E D . C A R R .
B I G T E N . N O T I M E
I N C A S E . H O R D E S
T O Y S . . . L O S E R S
```

PUZZLE 24

```
A D V . A C H E . B M O C
S E A . B U O Y . L I M A
T L C . I R R E G U L A R
R I C O T T A . H E N R Y
O L I V E . C L O S E S .
S A N E . B E A U . . . .
. H E R O D . S L O W S .
. . H A M S . P I T T . .
. P A P A Y A . D A L A I
C E D A R . D I A L S U P
A T O N E M E N T . O N T
P A R T . E D I E . N C O
O L E S . D O T S . S H E
```

```
  S M A R T S     C A L F
  L A W M A N     A G I R L
S I L E N C E     R O M E O
I P A D     K A E L     B U G
N O R     T Y K E     S O D S
A N I M E     S K I N
I S A I A H     S T O R M S
      C R I B     S W E E T
C E E S     N A S A     P R E
A M A     B D R M     C A G E
M O S S Y     R E C O V E R
E J E C T     E L O P E R
      I L I E     L L O Y D S
```

```
F I F E S         P O G O
A N O R A K     D U P O N T
S T O R M Y     I M P A I R
T E D       L P G A     T O Y
S N I F T E R S     F E N S
    T E L E     O I L I E S T
        A T T U N E D
R A G W E E D     W E L K
A C E S     M E D D L I N G
I C Y     S P R Y       M A E
D E S P O T     E N D I V E
S P E L L S     S A U T E S
    T R O D       P O S S E
```

```
      O R C A     L S D
U H S     W O O S     I C E
R O U T E O N E     M A T A
B R A W N     G A M B L E D
A D V I S E R     A S P C A
N E E R     T E N N     S T Y
      L A S S O E S
A D S     N Y S E     T A M E
L U C I D     I L L E G A L
V E R T I G O     L A I R S
A L O E     I N S O M N I A
    E L M     G A R Y     G A S
    R L S     S L I D
```

```
S T A R Z     O A T H S
T O M E I     S C R E E C H
O N I O N     C H A R L I E
R T S     C I A O     A T T A
M O S T     C R O C     Z I T
      A L E S     F L E E S
A U D I S     C O O R S
S R T A S     R A S P
A T E     A P E S     S A M S
G I N S     I D A S     B A A
A S S U M E D     E V E R T
S T I R F R Y     G O L D A
    L E A S E     A L L I N
```

```
    D W A R F S     C A P P
  M A R S A L A     P L E A
T A L I S M A N     O L E G
I B E T     B I G     O R E
E E E     C O L T     E V E S
S L A S H     S O I L E D
    R O E       S I R
  I N S T E P     L E T B E
S O H O     L U C E     H A T
A D A     E T A     M E L T
F I R M     C O N S O M M E
E N D S     T U E S D A Y
S E T S     S T R E E P
```

```
      M A L E     B O T H
S T O U T E R     A B R A
C O R S A G E     S A I N T
A N A T     R E M A K E
L E T A   C L I     A L I E
D R E N C H I N G     S E N
      G U E S S E D
A F B     P E P E L E P E W
S A L T     S S S     S E M I
S C U R R Y       P A C E
T A R O T     A P P A R E L
    D A V E     B R O I L E D
    E Y E S     S E E R
```

PUZZLE 31

```
S O B E   U F O S
A P E X   G O A T H E R D
H E L P   L A K E E R I E
A N T O N Y M   S A R G E
R E E S E       R E I D
A D D   B O A R   O D D S
      D R O P O F F
P I K E   P O O L   B E E
A N O N       A L E X A
C L A S P   I M P O R T S
T E L E V I S E   R A R E
S T A R T I N G   E T A L
      S I T S   N E S S
```

PUZZLE 32

```
    L I D S     A S P S
  S I N N E R   L E A H
S T O M A C H   L A P U P
T U N E     E M A N A T E
A D E   A C T I   P S S T
M I L K B O T T L E
P O S I E S   T O N G U E
    C L E V E R N E S S
E R I K   L I N D   M E T
R E C O I L S   R I S E
S T I F F   I N G E N U E
  R E F S   T U R N I P
  O R S O   B R O S
```

PUZZLE 33

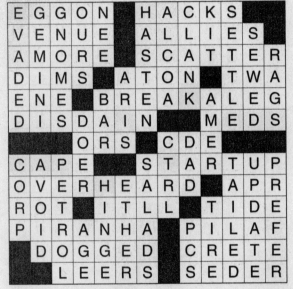

```
E G G O N   H A C K S
V E N U E   A L L I E S
A M O R E   S C A T T E R
D I M S   A T O N   T W A
E N E   B R E A K A L E G
D I S D A I N   M E D S
    O R S   C D E
C A P E   S T A R T U P
O V E R H E A R D   A P R
R O T   I T L L   T I D E
P I R A N H A   P I L A F
  D O G G E D   C R E T E
  L E E R S   S E D E R
```

PUZZLE 34

```
G A S P S     S H A M E
I N O I L   T E A T I M E
L E F T Y   R O L O D E X
A M T S   P I U S   N N E
S I S   N A T L   R I D S
  C H E E S E   B O G S
    E V A S   W I S H
  S L I P   C H A S T E
M A L L   K A Y S   S N L
T L C   M A G S   A N T I
N U R T U R E   C L A R A
S T A B L E S   R A C E R
  E B S E N   Y I K E S
```

PUZZLE 35

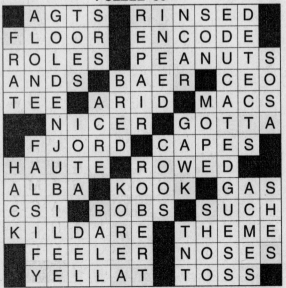

```
  A G T S   R I N S E D
F L O O R   E N C O D E
R O L E S   P E A N U T S
A N D S   B A E R   C E O
T E E   A R I D   M A C S
    N I C E R   G O T T A
  F J O R D   C A P E S
H A U T E   R O W E D
A L B A   K O O K   G A S
C S I   B O B S   S U C H
K I L D A R E   T H E M E
  F E E L E R   N O S E S
  Y E L L A T   T O S S
```

PUZZLE 36

```
  C H E A P   S L A M
  A A M C O   S A L O O N
  B L O C K   N O B O D Y
  B I T T E N   S U S I E
C A F E   F O B   M E E T
P G A   D U V E T S
R E X   U N I T E   C O P
    C H A C H A   A C E
A C M E   T E L   O V E N
P R I M E   S E R I A L
R E N E G E   H E L L O
S W I N G S   E B E R T
  S T O P   M A R Y S
```

PUZZLE 37

A	W	R	Y	■	■	S	T	A	I	R	■	■
D	R	O	O	P	■	M	O	U	T	H	S	■
D	O	Y	O	U	■	A	R	R	A	Y	E	D
E	T	C	■	S	E	R	T	A	■	M	A	A
D	E	E	■	H	A	T	E	■	H	E	R	R
■	■	■	U	P	S	Y	■	F	O	R	C	E
■	E	E	R	I	E	■	H	A	R	S	H	■
A	G	A	I	N	■	H	U	L	A	■	■	■
S	G	T	S	■	B	O	S	C	■	O	D	S
I	N	C	■	G	E	C	K	O	■	C	I	A
N	O	R	F	O	L	K	■	N	B	C	T	V
■	■	G	O	O	G	L	E	■	S	A	U	T	E
■	■	W	O	O	E	D	■	■	A	R	O	D

PUZZLE 38

■	■	C	H	O	W	■	R	A	P	I	D	S
■	P	O	A	C	H	■	O	U	I	O	U	I
■	R	O	U	T	E	■	B	R	E	W	E	D
■	A	L	L	S	E	T	■	E	R	A	S	E
B	I	N	■	■	■	A	D	V	■	■	■	■
O	R	E	O	S	■	G	E	O	R	G	E	S
D	I	S	H	E	S	■	C	I	N	E	M	A
Y	E	S	M	A	A	M	■	R	A	T	E	S
■	■	■	■	L	O	A	■	■	O	N	S	■
I	M	A	G	E	■	S	H	O	U	L	D	■
R	E	L	I	V	E	■	A	B	C	D	E	■
A	R	I	S	E	S	■	T	I	L	E	D	■
N	E	T	T	L	E	■	S	T	A	R	■	■

PUZZLE 39

■	T	I	M	S	■	■	A	C	A	R	E
■	O	N	R	A	M	P	■	D	U	P	E	D
L	O	G	I	C	A	L	■	D	E	P	T	S
E	L	M	S	■	S	O	W	S	■	L	I	E
A	A	A	■	O	T	T	O	■	P	E	E	L
S	T	R	A	W	■	S	N	O	U	T	■	■
H	E	B	R	E	W	■	T	H	R	U	S	H
■	■	E	F	R	O	N	■	M	E	R	C	I
S	E	R	S	■	R	I	C	E	■	N	E	D
A	L	G	■	F	E	L	L	■	A	O	N	E
S	I	M	B	A	■	E	V	O	L	V	E	S
S	T	A	L	L	■	S	I	P	P	E	R	■
Y	E	N	T	A	■	■	T	O	R	Y	■

PUZZLE 40

■	T	B	O	N	E	■	P	A	I	L	S	■
S	A	B	L	E	S	■	O	W	N	U	P	■
A	U	G	E	R	S	■	P	E	T	C	O	■
G	N	U	■	D	E	L	I	■	L	I	K	E
A	T	N	O	■	N	I	N	A	■	L	A	W
■	■	■	T	A	C	O	■	M	I	L	N	E
C	I	V	I	L	E	N	G	I	N	E	E	R
A	R	I	S	E	■	C	A	S	K	■	■	■
R	E	S	■	C	R	U	Z	■	S	P	A	Y
D	L	I	I	■	A	B	E	T	■	E	R	A
■	A	T	T	I	C	■	B	O	O	K	E	R
■	N	O	T	M	E	■	O	N	L	O	A	N
■	D	R	O	P	S	■	S	I	D	E	S	■

PUZZLE 41

■	T	O	R	S	O	■	D	I	S	C	O	■
C	E	L	T	I	C	■	A	L	L	A	N	■
A	S	S	E	R	T	■	B	L	U	N	T	■
A	L	E	■	S	O	L	O	■	G	N	A	W
N	A	N	A	■	B	I	N	D	■	O	R	R
■	■	■	D	I	E	T	■	Y	A	L	I	E
B	L	O	O	D	R	E	L	A	T	I	O	N
R	I	N	S	E	■	R	A	N	T	■	■	■
E	K	E	■	S	H	A	M	■	Y	I	P	S
W	E	T	S	■	E	L	E	M	■	N	R	A
■	N	I	E	C	E	■	N	O	T	F	A	R
■	E	M	A	I	L	■	T	R	A	U	M	A
■	D	E	L	I	S	■	S	T	U	N	S	■

PUZZLE 42

S	T	R	I	P	■	■	T	O	T	E	■
H	E	A	R	T	■	P	H	R	A	S	E	■
A	X	L	E	S	■	L	O	B	S	T	E	R
R	A	P	■	■	T	A	N	S	■	A	Y	E
I	N	H	A	L	I	N	G	■	S	T	O	W
■	■	■	W	O	M	B	■	T	H	E	R	E
D	A	M	A	G	E	■	R	E	U	S	E	D
I	L	I	K	E	■	N	U	N	S	■	■	■
E	L	S	E	■	H	O	T	S	H	O	T	S
G	U	S	■	M	U	S	S	■	■	W	O	O
O	R	I	G	A	M	I	■	S	A	N	K	A
■	E	L	I	X	I	R	■	S	H	E	E	P
■	E	N	I	D	■	■	W	A	R	N	S	■

PUZZLE 43

```
C L O G . . . B M W . . .
R A R E . R U L E . C D S
I S I N . E L L S . H R H
S T E E R A G E . L I I I
C O N S O L E . S A L V E
O F T . D I S B A N D E D
. . . M E G . L U G . . .
C O T T O N G I N . D D S
R U I N S . O N A D I E T
A T M S . A S K S O V E R
M D I . D U P E . R I P E
P O D . M R E D . K N E W
. . . V A L . . S E R S .
```

PUZZLE 44

```
. M I D A S . . P E A L E
. A F A R M . S E N S E D
. P I N T O . O C T A N E
. . C I O . H A R P O N .
M I N E S T R O N E . . .
E L M . T H E . S E C T S
T I E R . S I D . S I R E
S E X E S . G I S . A I L
. . S O U N D P R O O F .
A L I E N S . T A E . . .
L E A R N S . I D R I S .
D E N V E R . M E A N T .
A S S E T . . E D N A S .
```

PUZZLE 45

```
. F A T A L . G R E T A .
T E N U R E . R O Y A L .
W A N T A D . O N E P M .
A S I . B U R P . S I A M
S T E R . P E E P . O N A
. . . O A T S . V I C A R
R A I L R O A D T R A C K
A S N E R . L I S A . . .
M P H . S M E E . S L A T
S E E D . A S S T . E G O
. C R A W L . E R M I N E
. T I D A L . L U G G E D
. S T A R S . S E T H S .
```

PUZZLE 46

```
C N B C . A B A T . . .
H O R A . D O L E . S T P
I V A N . O B O E . C H A
D I V O T . B E T R A Y S
E C O N O M Y . H A R M S
D E S . R I M S . I S E E
. . L I N C O L N . . . .
A P S O . I F F Y . A P T
I R E N E . E A R A C H E
S I M I L A R . E L T O N
L E I . E C R U . T I N A
E S S . C L I P . E V E N
. . . T U N A . R E S T .
```

PUZZLE 47

```
. A H A S . C Z E C H .
. L E V I S . R A S H E S
T A M E S T . A P P E A L
A M A . T O U T . N E V E
C O N D E N S E . R I D .
. . O R E S . S K I E S .
. C A R L . M O O R . . .
A R R A Y . S L O B . . .
N U M . S T I L E T T O .
N E O N . L A N D . W H Y
A L I C I A . D E T A I L
S T R I C T . A R K I N .
. Y E S E S . S O N G . .
```

PUZZLE 48

```
S T A K E . P S A T S . .
A R E A L . L A G O O N .
S A I L S . A L T E R E R
H M O . R C A S . C E E .
. P U R S U E D . G E D S
. O H M S . B E R L E .
W A L L O P . N O T Y E T
A D E L E . L U L U . . .
N I T S . T E N T P E G .
D D T . S H E S . V I E .
S A U C I E R . E L I Z A
. S C O T I A . S E A M S
. E X E R T . C A N O E .
```

PUZZLE 49

```
    C A R A     A C A S T
  S E A L E D   N O R M A
  E X P A N D   G O T U P
A C C O S T S   L I S T S
D R I N K     B E N
L E S   A L M A   G I B E
I T E   N I N J A   N E B
B E D S   F O A L   S H O
      I N T     U N I O N
H A R P O   T I M I D L Y
I N E P T   R A N K E D
S A B E R   I G U E S S
S T A R E   M O S S
```

PUZZLE 50

```
D O R M   S G T S
A B E E   H O O P     A L S
Y A L L   E D G E     L I I
S M I T H   D O C K I N G
P A S S A G E   S E V E N
A S H   R O S E   Y E N S
    F I E S T A S
A C R E   S O A P   O M G
S L E E T   F L I P P E R
T O P S O I L   G E E N A
O N O   A N O N   A N D S
R E T   D I V A   S E E P
      S T E T   E R R S
```

PUZZLE 51

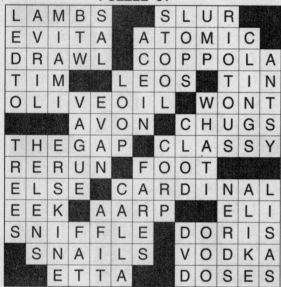

```
L A M B S   S L U R
E V I T A   A T O M I C
D R A W L   C O P P O L A
T I M   L E O S   T I N
O L I V E O I L   W O N T
    A V O N   C H U G S
T H E G A P   C L A S S Y
R E R U N   F O O T
E L S E   C A R D I N A L
E E K   A A R P   E L I
S N I F F L E   D O R I S
    S N A I L S   V O D K A
      E T T A   D O S E S
```

PUZZLE 52

```
    S O L A R   M O O S
    S T R I P E   S P U R T
S C A R L E T   A G I L E
O E R   T R A W L   J O E
U N T O   I R E L A N D
S I L L   A N A M E
A C E D   P I P   G O N E
    E A R N S   I R O N
S H I N D I G   T A M S
N A N   E L W A Y   T A U
A S T H E   A L A M O D E
C O R E R   L O W E R S
K N O T   L U N G S
```

PUZZLE 53

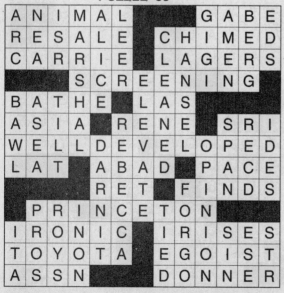

```
A N I M A L   G A B E
R E S A L E   C H I M E D
C A R R I E   L A G E R S
    S C R E E N I N G
B A T H E   L A S
A S I A   R E N E   S R I
W E L L D E V E L O P E D
L A T   A B A D   P A C E
    R E T   F I N D S
  P R I N C E T O N
I R O N I C   I R I S E S
T O Y O T A   E G O I S T
A S S N     D O N N E R
```

PUZZLE 54

```
O D E S     O R D E R
L I L T S   U S H E R E D
A L L O T   S A M U E L S
F L A M E   E L E N A
    P E R U   I M P S
J I F   P O P S   O I L S
E N L I S T   C A N N O T
S K I M   S T A B   G P S
T Y P E   O R C A
    P A B L O   D A M O N
A B A N D O N   E R I C A
D E N I A L S   F O R T Y
J E T T Y     N E S S
```

PUZZLE 55

```
. W R E A T H . M I C H .
. S H A M P O O . A F R O .
S P E C T R U M . P A I R .
H I R E . I R A . L S D
O R E . A L E G . P L I E
P O S T S . D E B I T S .
. T R I . C P O .
. C H A S E R . D E P O T
E L E M . R I D E . I V Y
L O B . R B I . L E A K
I V E S . O B S T A C L E
Z E E S . R O C K I E S .
A R F S . S N O O T S .
```

PUZZLE 56

```
C A S S . A R E A S .
A R O M A . G A R N E T
A M B L E D . I N M A T E
L E O . L E A R . A T T N
F O R E T E L L . O L D
. T I R E . A C M E S
. C M O N . D A Y S .
A L O N G . S O D A .
D O T . F E M I N I N E
A S H E . E X I T . T O W
P E E L E R . T I G H T S
T U R B A N . S O N A R .
. P S A T S . N U D E
```

PUZZLE 57

```
. P C S . S T E A M .
A L A R M . E A R L I E R
B O N E S . T O R O N T O
E G A D . M S S . H O H O
S I M I L E . C A R E T
. C A T E R S T O . S R S
. S A L T I N E .
R E G . F E S T I V A L
E L E G Y . A C I D I C
H U R L . T O N . C O C O
A D M I R E R . S T R I P
B E A D I N G . R E N T S
. N E O N S . A D S .
```

PUZZLE 58

```
A R C H . C L A S P .
E U R O S . A L B E R T
T R A P P . R A C C O O N
N A B . A T O M S . C F O
A L S . N O L A . H E F T
. A I D E . L O S E S
. E M B E D . T E N S E
S M A L L . S H A G .
A I R Y . E W E R . C A D
I N T . P R E E N . H E R
L E I S U R E . E R A S E
. M A S C O T . D E F O G
. L E E R S . P E P S
```

PUZZLE 59

```
. H A R M . A G E D .
C A T A L O G . C O M O
A D A M A N T . T R O U T
R I G S . T S E T S E
D E U T . S H H . D E E S
S U P E R H E R O . D D S
. R E E L I N G .
N B C . S E L F S E R V E
A A H S . N O T . T E A M
B L O O M S . L I L I
S L I D E . C O C O N U T
. A C O W . C L A S S E S
. D E M S . C E N T
```

PUZZLE 60

```
. D D T . S H E E T .
T I E U P . T O S S U P S
E M B E R . A U S T R I A
N P R . A F I R E . N N W
O L I V I E R . S M I T E
R E S I S T S . A P O D
. C E E . T A G .
S A S K . P E R I O D S
P L A I D . E A T C R O W
A M C . A W A R E . A M A
C A R A M E L . R O N A N
E Y E S O R E . Y O G I S
. D I N E D . H E N
```

```
■ ■ P E A ■ P I N E ■
S K I R T ■ A L L O F M E
L O C A L ■ H A L I F A X
I A N S ■ T O T ■ S O M E
E L I ■ T A Y E ■ I R I S
R A C K E T S ■ T E T E ■
■ ■ A A A ■ H R S ■ ■
■ C A R S ■ S O O T H E D
S H U E ■ S C O T ■ E G O
C O N N ■ T E D ■ R A G U
A R T I S A N ■ H E R O S
T E E N A G E ■ A L O N E
■ ■ M A T S ■ ■ N S F ■
```

```
■ ■ T U L S A ■ I S A A C
■ B A T M A N ■ V A N C E
P I M E N T O ■ S P A I N
A L P ■ O A R S ■ ■ M D S
D L I I ■ N A N N I E S ■
R E N D S ■ K I C K ■ ■
E D G I E R ■ T O N S I L
■ ■ O L E S ■ S O U S A
■ C U T L E T S ■ W I L T
D A N ■ D U O S ■ T A T
A F I N E ■ A B A L O N E
R E F I T ■ R E G A R D ■
N S Y N C ■ T R A P S ■
```

```
■ ■ D E M O ■ B E L L E
B L O W U P S ■ A V A I L
R E N E G E D ■ C A N E S
E A T S ■ R A S H ■ D U I
A R M ■ S A K E ■ M O T E
K N E L T ■ C L E F ■ ■
■ S N O U T ■ T O I L S ■
■ ■ T I N E ■ G R I E F
M R I S ■ C A G E ■ N N E
O O O ■ W H I R ■ N C A A
R A N C H ■ R E B O O T S
S N I D E ■ S T A R L E T
E S T E E ■ A M A N ■
```

```
O F A L L ■ A D D I N ■
M A D E A ■ L I O N E L
A I L E D ■ P E N C I L S
R N A ■ M A T T ■ T A E
■ T I C T A C S ■ A H M E
■ Y O G A ■ B L E A T
G R A N T S ■ E V E R S O
L E V I S ■ C M D R ■
O P E C ■ W H I S T L E
S A N ■ B A I T ■ I A N
S I G M U N D ■ B I N G O
■ D E C R E E ■ F I E L D
■ R I N D S ■ F I R E S
```

```
■ G N A W ■ L A M P S ■
■ R E T R O ■ O M E L E T
H A R M E D ■ A S T U T E
M I V ■ C D E F ■ E M T S
S N E A K E R S ■ P E T
■ ■ T I R E ■ C L U E S
■ C M O N ■ O O P S ■
C L A N G ■ M O L L ■ ■
H I S ■ B I G E A T E R
A C C T ■ O A R S ■ A B E
S H A W L S ■ E L O P E D
M E R I T S ■ S A F E R ■
■ S A N D Y ■ W A R T ■
```

```
■ N A A C P ■ F G H I
■ G E I S H A ■ S A R A H
O N T R I A L ■ P R O V O
R O W ■ S I M B A ■ P E P
B M O C ■ N E O N ■ E N S
S E R V E ■ R O N A ■ ■
■ S K I N S ■ B E R L E
■ ■ I D L E ■ R I O T S
A C T ■ E E L S ■ Z A C H
B A A ■ A D E P T ■ T H O
E N T E R ■ C R U S H E D
A D A M S ■ T A N K E R ■
T O S S ■ S T A Y S ■
```

PUZZLE 67

```
  T W I T     B A W L S  
E R I C A   Y A H O O S  
T U C K S   G R O U C H O
A C H Y   L O O M   I O N
L E I   M I N N   F A R M
    T H E M E   A L L E Y
  L A I N E   C R O S S  
D U K E S   A Z T E C    
E G A D   A L A S   I D S
A N N   W H I R   D E E M
D U S T R A G   M O N T E
  T A V E R N   E M C E E
    S A N D S   L E E R  
```

PUZZLE 68

```
      T I N A   S C A R S
P R O V E R B   O I L E R
L A Y E T T E   D I G I T
A D O S   I A N S   O N A
N A T   T E T E   I R I S
B R A K E   L E S S E N  
        A D D E D O N    
  B A L S A M   S T A L L
C E D E   T A R O   E I O
U M A   B A N E   T R O D
T I P S Y   I S S U I N G
U N T I E   A I R B A S E
P E S T S   N O E L      
```

PUZZLE 69

```
  T A M P A   S T R E P  
I C E B E R G   C H I V E
N O M A D I C   R E S E T
A S P   A M Y   O M E N S
S T E E L   F L I N T    
E A R N S   W E L K      
C R A G   G A Y   A S T O
    I B M S   A D L I B  
  D U N E S   M O O D S  
R E L E T   A C E   P I E
O C T E T   R A L L I E S
B A R R Y   F R I E N D S
B L A S S   S L A N G    
```

PUZZLE 70

```
  A P E D   S T E A L    
C L I P O N   C O B R A S
A T T I R E   A T B E S T
P E A C E T I M E   A S A
O R S   M T N   M E R I T
      L I E N   R U E S  
  Y O O   D I M   L G S  
C O R A   N O P E        
R U I N S   G R R   M F A
A R G   C A S T O R O I L
C E A S E D   A B O U N D
K I M O N O   R E D S E A
  T I N T S   D E E D    
```

PUZZLE 71

```
A A R P   A T R I U M    
G H O U L   C L E A N S E
T O M E I   A M E N D E D
S T A R Z   T A U T      
    T A B S   P E A L S  
O K C O R R A L   D L I I
I W O   D I N A H   O M G
L A N A   E D M O N T O N
S I E V E   D A L I      
    I T T O   D E L T A  
R O A D H O G   I C I E R
C A L L E R S   T E A S E
A R G Y L E     S R T A  
```

PUZZLE 72

```
I T H A D   I M S O      
T H E S E   G I A N T S  
S O D A F O U N T A I N S
A R G   M A E S   L E A  
N E A T E N S   P I E R  
    G A G A   D A N Z A  
M A Z O L A   B E R G E N
A B O N E   M I C E      
R U D Y   R E T O R T S  
C S I   H I R E   R A P  
H E A D O V E R H E E L S
  S C O P E S   O R E O S
    W I T T   W A S N T  
```

PUZZLE 73

E	R	E		C	H	U	M		T	S	K	S
D	E	C		N	A	S	A		O	H	N	O
I	S	L	A	N	D	E	R		P	R	A	M
C	O	A	L		E	R	I	C		A	C	E
T	R	I	B	E	S		S	L	I	N	K	
	T	R	E	Y		S	K	U	N	K	S	
		R	E	H	E	A	T	S				
	A	C	T	I	O	N		C	U	R	T	
M	O	A	N	A		T	H	R	O	A	T	
O	I	L		G	R	A	Y		E	Y	R	E
A	G	O	G		D	U	S	T	R	A	G	S
H	O	N	E		E	T	O	N		L	E	T
U	S	S	R		D	O	N	T		S	T	Y

PUZZLE 74

D	A	R	E		A	F	A	R		I	S	A
I	C	E	D		L	A	N	E		N	A	N
S	U	B	S		P	I	N	C	H	H	I	T
C	R	E	E	K		R	A	D	I	A	L	S
	A	L	L	E	G	E		P	L	O	Y	
			P	U	R	R		P	E	R		
	A	P	P	T	S		A	L	O	S	S	
	F	R	A		T	O	G	A				
A	F	I	T		P	E	W	T	E	R		
M	I	S	T	A	K	E		N	A	M	E	D
B	R	O	I	L	I	N	G		C	O	L	A
L	M	N		B	A	U	M		O	T	I	S
E	S	S		A	S	P	S		S	E	T	H

PUZZLE 75

I	N	F	O	R	M		C	T	R	L		
C	O	R	N	E	A		L	E	V	E	R	S
E	D	I	S	O	N		I	N	S	T	E	P
S	S	N		U	R	I	S		S	S	A	
		G	C	L	E	F		I	M	I	N	
	H	E	R	A	L	D		B	R	A	D	S
	O	B	E	Y		Y	O	K	E			
F	L	E	E	S		A	T	O	N	E	D	
R	E	N	D		L	I	B	Y	A			
E	S	E		P	E	T	A		D	D	S	
D	U	F	F	E	L		R	O	M	E	O	S
S	P	I	L	L	S		A	U	L	A	I	T
		T	A	T	E		S	T	I	L	T	S

PUZZLE 76

E	S	S	A	Y	S			O	R	G		
N	O	U	G	A	T	S		D	E	A	L	T
C	A	L	O	R	I	E		S	T	R	E	W
O	P	T		D	R	A	G		A	L	A	I
R	E	A	M	S		S	M	I	L	I	N	G
E	D	N	A			E	R	I	C	S		
			T	E	A		N	R	A			
	S	O	R	R	Y			T	I	D	E	
U	M	P	I	R	E	S		V	E	N	O	M
S	E	E	M		S	A	R	I		S	U	M
M	A	N	O	R		V	E	R	B	O	S	E
A	R	E	N	A		E	P	A	U	L	E	T
		D	Y	E		O	L	D	E	S	T	

PUZZLE 77

	O	S	L	O		M	A	P	S			
A	D	R	I	A	N		C	A	R	L	A	
B	O	A	R	D	I	N	G	H	O	U	S	E
A	N	T	I		C	O	W	S		M	S	S
T	O	O		D	E	S	I		S	P	E	C
E	R	R	E	D		E	R	N	E	S	T	
		L	A	G		E	O	N				
	J	E	K	Y	L	L		A	D	O	P	T
R	U	N	S		E	A	C	H		C	H	A
D	D	T		F	A	I	R		R	E	I	N
S	A	R	C	A	S	T	I	C	A	L	L	Y
	S	E	I	K	O		M	I	M	O	S	A
	E	V	E	N		P	O	S	T			

PUZZLE 78

	M	A	M	A	S		A	T	H	E	N	A
H	A	V	A	N	A		D	I	A	L	E	D
O	N	I	O	N	S		A	F	R	A	I	D
M	I	A		O	H	M		F	I	L	L	S
E	T	T	A			A	B	A				
R	O	O	M		B	E	R	N	A	R	D	
	B	R	O	A	D	W	A	Y	J	O	E	
	A	S	S	U	R	E	D		A	T	T	Y
			S	M	S		R	A	R	E		
A	B	E	E	T		T	O	T		T	A	S
L	A	D	L	E	S		P	O	L	I	C	E
P	L	I	E	R	S		A	G	E	N	T	S
S	I	E	V	E	S		L	O	N	G	S	

PUZZLE 79

	C	L	E	F	S		C	O	T	E	
	H	O	G	A	N		T	H	R	I	L	L
	A	D	O	R	E		Y	E	A	R	L	Y
O	M	G		M	A	P	L	E	L	E	A	F
R	B	I		S	K	I	E	R		S	S	T
C	E	N	T		P	R	I	G				
A	R	G	U	E	R		S	O	O	T	H	E
		E	X	E	S			T	O	I	L
M	F	A		P	A	R	I	S		A	S	I
B	A	R	C	E	L	O	N	A		S	T	S
A	B	D	U	C	T		A	L	I	T	O	
S	L	E	E	T	Y		N	E	V	E	R	
	E	N	D	S			E	M	E	R	Y	

PUZZLE 80

M	A	J	O	R			P	L	A	C	E	
A	L	E	V	E		D	I	P	L	O	M	A
S	C	R	A	P		R	E	G	I	M	E	N
K	A	R	L		D	O	R	A		M	R	T
S	P	Y		P	R	O	S		C	O	G	S
	P	O	R	T	A	L		L	O	N	E	
	C	O	A	T		L	A	R	D		
	T	O	T	S		K	I	D	D	I	E	
C	I	N	C		B	O	A	S		V	A	N
U	R	N		G	E	R	M		N	I	T	E
S	E	E	H	E	R	E		P	O	S	S	E
P	O	L	E	N	T	A		A	L	O	U	D
	F	L	E	A	S		C	A	R	P	S	

PUZZLE 81

	P	A	C	T	S		T	A	M	P
W	O	R	S	H	I	P	S		O	N	E	A
H	O	U	S	E	T	O	P		A	N	D	I
O	D	D		F	L	O	R	I	D	I	A	N
O	L	E		E	K	E	S		E	L	S	
P	E	N	S		D	Y	E	R	S		
I	S	T	O			I	T	A	L
	P	O	L	K	A		D	A	D	A
S	O	D		W	O	N	T		R	E	C
W	H	I	T	E	S	A	L	E		T	S	K
I	A	G	O		E	V	A	L	U	A	T	E
G	R	I	M		R	E	S	I	G	N	E	D
S	A	N	E		S	T	A	G	S	

PUZZLE 82

	M	I	M	E	S		P	H	I	L
	C	A	M	E	R	A		M	A	U	D	E
B	U	R	P	I	N	G		O	L	S	E	N
R	S	T		R	I	G	O	R		K	A	N
I	T	I	S		E	E	K	S		S	L	Y
B	O	N	U	S		D	R	E	W		
E	M	I	N	E	M		A	L	A	S	K	A
		S	C	A	B		S	N	A	I	L
A	R	C		R	I	L	E		T	Y	P	E
S	E	E		E	M	E	N	D		S	P	R
P	L	A	I	T		A	S	O	F	Y	E	T
C	A	S	T	S		C	U	T	T	E	R	
A	X	E	S		H	E	E	D	S	

PUZZLE 83

	T	B	S	P		B	A	G	S	
I	D	I	O	T	I	C		E	L	L	I	S
M	O	N	G	R	E	L		N	O	I	S	Y
P	O	P		U	S	A		C	E	N	T	S
E	N	A	C	T		R	A	H		D	E	T
L	E	N	O		C	A	F	E	C	A	R	
		P	L	O		A	S	A		
	S	P	E	E	D	E	R		K	O	P	S
S	O	L		S	E	W		C	Y	C	L	E
P	R	E	P	S		O	N	O		T	A	U
A	T	A	L	E		K	O	R	E	A	N	S
R	E	S	I	N		S	T	A	R	V	E	S
	D	E	E	S		E	L	S	E	

PUZZLE 84

		T	U	B	A		S	C	A	M	S
L	I	L	Y	P	A	D		R	O	S	I	E
E	M	E	R	A	L	D		S	P	I	C	E
A	P	S	O		S	O	B		Y	A	R	D
V	A	L		L	A	I	R		E	N	O	S
E	R	I	C	A		L	A	P	D		
S	T	E	A	K	S		N	O	I	S	E	S
		R	E	N	E		S	T	A	M	P
B	A	J	A		I	T	R	Y		F	O	E
A	L	U	M		T	H	E		T	A	T	E
D	A	L	E	Y		I	G	N	O	R	E	D
A	M	I	L	E		C	A	N	D	I	D	S
T	O	A	S	T		S	L	E	D	

PUZZLE 85

```
I D A S . . . S H A R P S
T I P T O P . T E P E E S
E V E R S O . A R L E N E
M E D A L S . N O U N . .
. . N O T A . I S L E S .
B O N D . U S M C . I T A
A L E . A R I E S . S T Y
R A G . R E D S . P T A S
A F L A C . E S A U . . .
. I C A N . A M B L E D .
P A G O D A . G A L O R E
O M E L E T . E N I G M A
T S E T S E . . C O A L .
```

PUZZLE 86

```
. . . G R U B . . O P T S
. M O I N E S . T R I P .
R E D C O A T . T O D A Y
A L D A . A V O C A D O .
P O E . I S L E . E L E M
I N S I S T E N C E . . .
D I S N E Y . D O D G E S
. . F E L L O W S H I P .
C A M E . E A R L . E L I
P O O R E S T . C R E E .
A R T I E . T W E A K E D
. T O O L . E A T S I N .
. A R R S . S C A N . . .
```

PUZZLE 87

```
. G O U R D S . A V A . .
L E F T O U T . C L O D S
I N F E R N O . O L I V E
M E L . Y E W . R E L I C
I R I S . . . A N N A L S
T I N A . B A B E . . . .
S C E N T E D C A N D L E
. . . O N E S . A R I A .
S C A L P S . . G A B S .
H I T U P . U M P . F R I
A G I R L . C O A S T A L
M A M I E . L O T T E R Y
. R E D . . A S H L E Y .
```

PUZZLE 88

```
B T W . A C T I . A Y E S
A R I . P A Y S . L I M O
R A N D O L P H . A P B S
N I N E . M E M E . P E A
S T I N G S . A F T E R .
S E M I . D E F I E S . .
. . A B S A L O M . . . .
H A R L E Y . R E A L . .
A S K E R . S T O P U P .
A N S . T I C K . U R G E
T G I F . A V I A T I O N
T O G O . L I L T . L S D
A N N O . S I L O . S I S
```

PUZZLE 89

```
A B C D E . S I L T . . .
N O H O W . T R I U M P H
G R A C E . R E S T O R E
E R R S . L A N A . V I I
L O L . N O P E . S I N S
. W I D E N S . R H E T T
. . E A V E . F O A M . .
W A S T E . P L A Q U E .
A C H E . I R A N . S N L
T A E . A C O W . Z I T I
T R E A S O N . P E C A N
S E N D I N G . B R A I D
. . S A S S . J O L L Y .
```

PUZZLE 90

```
S P I K E . . G O B A D .
L I N E U P . A D E L E .
A L T A R S . R E E L S .
B E R N . A N Y . R T E S
. D O U G L A S . C O R E
. . . E M T . . A L V A .
P A G A N S . D A N D E R
A C E S . D E M . . . . .
W H O S . C I T I Z E N .
S I R I . O N A . I V A N
. E G G O N . I N L O V E
. S I N C E . L O C K E R
. T A S T Y . S H E L F .
```

T	R	A	M	P		D	R	I	F	T	S	
S	O	N	A	R		E	A	S	I	E	R	
K	A	T	I	E		C	H	U	R	N	S	
	M	I	N	D	E	R		P	M	S		
		S	I	T	E				P	F	C	
A	T	T	A	C	H	E	S		B	E	A	U
T	A	H	I	T	I		P	A	R	E	N	T
O	R	A	L		C	O	O	L	I	D	G	E
N	A	N			B	O	G	S				
	K	L	M		S	K	E	T	C	H		
	A	Y	E	A	Y	E		B	L	O	O	M
H	O	A	X	E	S		R	E	P	O	T	
A	U	D	I	T	S		A	S	S	T	S	

	A	N	A	T		R	S	V	P	S	
	A	N	I	M	E		A	W	A	I	T	S
E	N	G	L	I	S	H	S	E	T	T	E	R
R	T	E		S	L	I	C	E		A	P	T
E	L	L	A		A	S	A	P		S	S	A
C	E	O	S			S	L	U	M		
T	R	U	S	S			P	O	N	C	E	
	N	E	A	T		S	E	A	L		
G	M	C		M	A	R	E		S	I	R	S
A	A	H		I	R	A	Q	I		G	M	A
P	U	L	L	N	O	P	U	N	C	H	E	S
S	L	O	G	A	N		A	S	P	E	N	
	S	E	E	R	S		L	O	A	D	

	M	A	D	A	M	E		L	I	T	U	P
	A	N	N	U	A	L		A	F	I	N	E
O	R	G	A	N	Z	A		S	E	M	I	S
R	Y	E		T	E	L		S	E	E	T	O
A	L	L	I	S		C	O	L	D	S	
L	O	I	N		S	H	O	E		
B	U	C	K	I	N	G	B	R	O	N	C	O
	M	A	T	S		R	E	A	P	
	T	R	A	P	P		E	B	E	R	T
T	H	E	R	E		S	N	L		D	E	E
A	R	R	I	D		T	O	T	A	L	E	D
R	O	U	S	E		E	L	O	P	E	R	
O	W	N	E	D		M	A	N	O	R	S	

	S	T	U	N	T		T	E	E	M	
	L	A	S	S	I	E		I	T	S	A	
	O	B	E	Y	E	D		M	O	T	I	F
S	W	O	R	N		G	R	E	N	A	D	E
R	E	O		C	H	A	O	S		T	E	A
O	R	S	O		A	R	G	U	M	E	N	T
	A	S	H		U	P	A		
D	E	C	R	E	A	S	E		A	B	B	A
A	D	A		C	H	O	S	E		E	R	R
V	I	R	T	U	A	L		D	F	L	A	T
E	T	H	E	R		O	R	D	A	I	N	
	H	O	L	E		S	O	I	L	E	D	
	S	P	E	D		B	E	A	D	S	

	C	A	M		A	L	O	U	
D	I	L	L	S		C	R	O	P	P	E	D
O	C	E	A	N		O	B	S	E	R	V	E
Y	E	A	S		B	U	Y		N	O	E	S
O	U	T		H	I	P	S		W	O	R	K
U	P	S	C	A	L	E		C	I	T	Y	
	O	R	E		B	A	D		
	F	G	H	I		T	O	N	E	S	U	P
D	A	R	E		S	I	T	S		E	N	E
U	B	E	R		M	E	H		E	D	I	T
S	L	E	E	P	E	R		E	L	A	T	E
K	E	N	N	E	L	S		H	I	K	E	S
	S	T	A	T		S	E	A	

	A	D	D	S		R	A	F	T	
	P	H	A	R	A	O	H		E	L	I	A
P	R	O	V	I	N	C	E		I	L	L	S
R	A	K	E	D		L	E	G	U	M	E	
I	D	E	S		C	O	L	A	N	D	E	R
G	A	Y		J	O	N		T	E	E	D	
	F	A	N	C	I	E	D		
	C	A	A	N		U	R	N		M	O	B
L	E	T	M	E	S	E	E		Y	O	W	L
E	N	T	I	T	Y		B	E	R	E	T	
A	S	A	N		R	E	L	A	T	O	R	S
P	U	C	E		U	R	C	H	I	N	S	
T	S	K	S		P	A	D	S	

PUZZLE 97

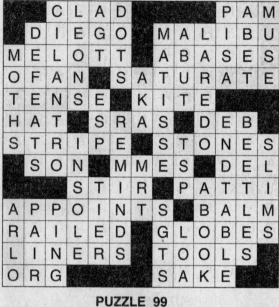

```
    C L A D       P A M
    D I E G O   M A L I B U
M E L O T T   A B A S E S
O F A N   S A T U R A T E
T E N S E   K I T E
H A T   S R A S   D E B
S T R I P E   S T O N E S
  S O N   M M E S   D E L
    S T I R   P A T T I
A P P O I N T S   B A L M
R A I L E D   G L O B E S
L I N E R S   T O O L S
O R G       S A K E
```

PUZZLE 98

```
M A C E       G O M E Z
A M P L E   P U R P O S E
Y E A R N   O M I T T E D
A S S O C   P A T I O
    Y O K E   C R E W
A L F   R A S H   A I D A
B A R K E R   A L L S E T
E V E N   L I I I   T N T
E A S E   C R A G
    H E I D I   B A S I C
C O M P A R E   L L A M A
C L E A N E R   E A T A T
L E N D S       S E N S
```

PUZZLE 99

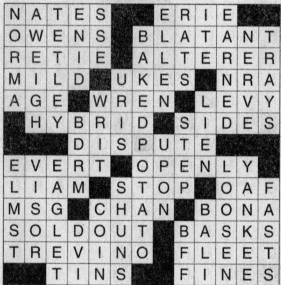

```
N A T E S   E R I E
O W E N S   B L A T A N T
R E T I E   A L T E R E R
M I L D   U K E S   N R A
A G E   W R E N   L E V Y
  H Y B R I D   S I D E S
      D I S P U T E
E V E R T   O P E N L Y
L I A M   S T O P   O A F
M S G   C H A N   B O N A
S O L D O U T   B A S K S
T R E V I N O   F L E E T
    T I N S   F I N E S
```

PUZZLE 100

```
  I N T A C T   N A N A
  S O R R O W   I D O L S
  A N E M I A   M A R I E
      S I N S   O G D E N
I N A S E C   A Y E S
R E D E S I G N   T K O
I A M S   D O G   C R E W
S R I   E V E R Y O N E
  R E N D   L E M M O N
S C A R E   A H A B
E L B O W   P A L A C E
W I L D E   P I L L O W
  P E E R   T R Y S T S
```

PUZZLE 101

```
  G A T O R   V E G A S
  D E L U D E   I R I S H
L A T I N O S   T E R S E
E K E   A R U B A   L E E
G O V T   S L A M   S T R
S T E A M   T R I G
  A N T E S   S N O O P
    A L E C   C A R L A
M T V   O M A R   D I A L
E E E   D I V O T   O C D
M E R C I   O P H E L I A
O U N C E   R E E L E D
S P E C S   T R A M S
```

PUZZLE 102

```
  S W I S S   G E R M
  S E A R C H   E V I A N
B A L L R O O M D A N C E
L I L T   W O O S   S A O
A G O   E L E V   S E W N
S O F A R   D I S K
E N F O L D   E R E C T S
    K E R R   A W A R E
S G T S   A I M S   P O X
P O W   D I V A   M L L E
C O O L O N E S H E E L S
A D A Y S   R O A S T S
  S M E E   A N N A S
```

PUZZLE 103

```
. G P A . S L U M . .
S T E E P . W I N E S A P
A R I A S . E T A G E R E
M I S L E A D . R A V E R
M P H . . S E A M . E A T
Y E A R . I N T E R N S .
. . A D M . T D S .
. T A P I O C A . T I L T
M A C . C V I I . P I E
A B E E T . G N A S H E S
A L I B A B A . S H O O T
S E N A T O R . S U N N Y
. . Y E P S . N N E
```

PUZZLE 104

```
A N T E S . S T A F F
S Y R I A . D A W D L E
S C U F F . E R O D E D
. M F A . L O S S E S
P E P P E R M I N T .
A L E . L I I . G E A R S
P A S T . S A L . P L I E
A L O H A . M E T . A C E
. I R R I G A T I O N
A M A N D A . I K E
R O C K E T . B E A D S
A L L E N S . L I C I T
B L U R T . E T H E L
```

PUZZLE 105

```
B T U S . I R S .
L I N K . N H L . T A T S
A T T Y . C O A C H M A N
S A I L O R . P U E B L O
S N E A K E D . T I L E R
. B R A I D . R E N E
H A S . A S K I N . S T S
O N T V . E E R I E
L Y R I C . S E N D F O R
D O U B T S . C A M A R O
I N T E R N E T . O L G A
T E S S . U T E . N C A R
. B C D . D O N S
```

PUZZLE 106

```
C L E A R . C A S S .
H A N D S . A B S O R B S
E P C O T . R U N S O U T
S T Y . U M P S . A B R A
S O C K . T E E D . E K G
. P L I A N T . O G R E S
. O W L S . T O R T .
H O P I S . A R M A D A
O N E . O K L A . Y E N S
R I D E . N Y P D . N E T
D O I L I E S . A N I M E
E N A B L E S . T U R I N
. A L L A . A M O C O
```

PUZZLE 107

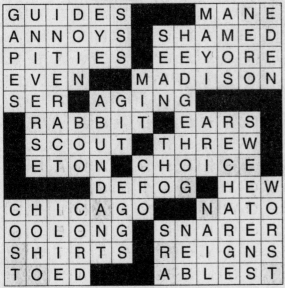

```
G U I D E S . M A N E
A N N O Y S . S H A M E D
P I T I E S . E E Y O R E
E V E N . M A D I S O N
S E R . A G I N G .
. R A B B I T . E A R S
. S C O U T . T H R E W
. E T O N . C H O I C E
. . D E F O G . H E W
C H I C A G O . N A T O
O O L O N G . S N A R E R
S H I R T S . R E I G N S
T O E D . A B L E S T
```

PUZZLE 108

```
I C E C A P . A D A G E
F I G A R O . C O C O A
S T O R M S . H U R L S
. N O T A . B O D Y
L A S E R . B A L S A
I L A Y . L I N E S M A N
M E T . W E L D S . E L I
B E E H I V E S . H I L T
. L O G I N . M A R Y S
. S L U G . E R I N .
A I S L E . I G N O R E
S T E E R . S H A D E S
H E D D A . E T H E L S
```